MUSIC AND THE POWER OF SOUND

Other books by Alain Daniélou
(in English)

Gods of Love and Ecstasy:
The Traditions of Shiva and Dionysus
Inner Traditions International, Rochester, Vermont, 1992

Manimekhalai: The Dancer with the Magic Bowl
Merchant-Prince Shatan, translated from the Tamil by Alain Daniélou
and T. V. Gopala Iyer,
New Directions, New York, 1989

Myths and Gods of India
Inner Traditions International, Rochester, Vermont, 1991

The Phallus
Inner Traditions International, Rochester, Vermont, 1995

The Ragas of Northern Indian Music
Reprint, Munshiram Manoharlal, New Delhi, 1980

Shilappadikaram (The Ankle Bracelet)
Prince Llango Adigal, translated from the Tamil, New Directions,
New York, 1965

Virtue, Success, Pleasure, and Liberation:
The Four Aims of Life in the Tradition of Ancient India
Inner Traditions International, Rochester, Vermont, 1993

The Way to the Labyrinth: Memories of East and West
New Directions, New York, 1987

While the Gods Play:
Shaiva Oracles and Predictions on the Cycles of
History and the Destiny of Mankind
Inner Traditions International, Rochester, Vermont, 1987

Yoga: Mastering the Secrets of Matter and the Universe
Inner Traditions International, Rochester, Vermont, 1991

MUSIC AND THE POWER OF SOUND

The Influence of Tuning and Interval on Consciousness

Alain Daniélou

Inner Traditions
Rochester, Vermont

Inner Traditions International
One Park Street
Rochester, Vermont 05767

First published as *Introduction to the Study of Musical Scales* by
the India Society, London, 1943.

Revised edition first published by Inner Traditions International, 1995.

LIBRARY OF CONGRESS CATALOGING-IN-PUBLICATION DATA
Daniélou, Alain.
Music and the power of sound : the influence of tuning and interval on
consciousness / Alain Daniélou.
p.   cm.
Rev. ed. of : Introduction to the study of musical scales. 1943.
Includes bibliographical references and index.
ISBN 0-89281-336-9
1. Musical intervals and scales. 2. Music—Philosophy and aesthetics.
I. Daniélou, Alain. Introduction to the study of musical scales. II. Title.
ML 3812.D28   1994
781.2'46–dc20   89–19876
                                                                CIP
Printed and bound in the United States

10 9 8 7 6 5 4 3 2 1

Text design and charts by Charlotte Tyler
This book was set in Janson with Anna and Cochin as display faces

Distributed to the book trade in Canada
by Publishers Group West (PGW), Toronto, Ontario
Distributed to the book trade in the United Kingdom by Deep Books, London
Distributed to the book trade in Australia by
Millennium Books, Newtown, N.S.W.
Distributed to the book trade in New Zealand by
Tandem Books, Auckland

To Max d'Ollone
and
Śivendranāth Basu

CONTENTS

~ *Chapter One* ~

METAPHYSICAL CORRESPONDENCES

~ *Chapter Two* ~

THE CONFLICT OF MUSICAL SYSTEMS

~ *Chapter Three* ~

THE MEASUREMENT OF INTERVALS AND HARMONIC SOUNDS

~ *Chapter Six* ~

CONFUSION OF THE SYSTEMS: THE MUSIC OF THE GREEKS

~ *Chapter Seven* ~

THE WESTERN SCALE AND EQUAL TEMPERAMENT

~ *Chapter Eight* ~

THE SCALE OF SOUNDS

TABLES AND FIGURES

FOREWORD

The musicological work of Alain Daniélou must be seen in a particular light since he happens to be by nature a musician. This is by no means common. How many musicologists, even the most famous, are not musicians! How many, indeed, are antimusical to the point of embodying the very negation of what constitutes a musician!

This is why I was wondering how Daniélou could be a musicologist, since he is a philosopher, a gifted linguist, a writer, a delightful painter, a composer, and an artist. This last quality is so obvious in him that it includes all the others. The sum of so many distinguished achievements reflects nothing more nor less than an equal sum of hard work.

Though it might seem irrelevant, I should like to compare the construction of an inner being, worked out with patience, method, and application during a long and generous life, to the cross-section of an architectural design, which perhaps reveals a difficulty solved through an ingenious device. Even if such a solution appears an inspiration or a gift of grace, it remains linked to a constant life of study.

All this being said, there is nothing surprising in the fact that Daniélou's approach should be completely his own, following completely unconventional lines—lines that are new and unexplored, and that may appear inaccessible or even hostile. There is no question of shortcuts nor of the rediscovery of ancient roads long abandoned.

Daniélou's inquiry is typically scientific. It cannot be seen as a continuation of previous work. It is strictly current and completely modern, and in many cases its conclusions appear definitive. They are presented here in one short work of a moral value worthy of Leopardi, covering a field that would normally require several inflated volumes from Doctors of Music, in which they would develop the most boring theories.

Daniélou attacks the immobility of the West from the perspective of the Far East. From there, it is paradoxically the West that appears to be a static and contemplative world, one that has been asleep for millenia. The substance of his theories rests on an experience, deeper than one might imagine, of the essence of music as it is found in the East. He confronts us with an irrefutable critique of the many artificial deformations of music's original language, showing how the fact of consonance as understood in the ancient world, and as it has been kept alive in Indian music, reveals unexplored possibilities.

Composers of our time would do well to explore the intricate but transparent routes of the labyrinth of sounds, and study attentively the inner implications of this important book.

In the second chapter, Daniélou's reflections on timbre and the choice of particular instruments are especially valuable; he seems to be the only one to underline the fundamental distinction between musical sounds and sounds that in fact are not musical. This crucial parameter has obvious implications in most aspects of present-day music. We read how harmonics are usually but not always multiples of the fundamental frequency. Instruments such as the violin or accordion produce, together with each note, a large number of harmonics, often louder than the note itself; other instruments such as the flute or the isolated string of a piano possess relatively few audible harmonics. Each sound forms with its own harmonics a complex chord possessing in itself a precise meaning. One often hears stupidities from people incapable of observation; it is with relief that one reads these considerations of luminous clarity about facts we tend to ignore but which represent a sacred and attractive threshold. This is the first marble step of an ascent toward the revelation of a higher world; a magic carpet near which we take off our shoes, ready to enter the sidereal space of liberated sound.

Sylvano Bussotti
Rome, January 1989

EDITOR'S NOTE

Music and the Power of Sound was first published under the title *Introduction to the Study of Musical Scales* in London in 1943. The author's own French translation was published in France in 1959 under the title *Traité de musicologie comparée* and has recently been reprinted. Despite the publication in India in 1969 of an unauthorized facsimile of the original edition, however, the book has been virtually unobtainable in English in the West since the 1943 edition went out of print. On a trip to India in 1987, I discovered the Indian edition of the book and devoured it at one sitting on a train journey from Delhi to Bombay. Here, it seemed to me, was someone who was answering with clarity and precision many of the questions that had been preoccupying me concerning the nature of music and its power to evoke in us feelings and images. It was an approach both universal and specific, one that made sense of the cultural differences between musical forms as well as the underlying threads that link them all.

Through the International Institute for Comparative Musicology in Berlin, of which Alain Daniélou was the founder, I contacted him at his home in Italy. He was delighted when I proposed republishing this valuable work and making it once again readily available in English.

This edition has been fully revised and rendered into more modern English, with the approval and cooperation of the author. It was perhaps part of the charm of the original edition that it was written in English by a Frenchman living in India, but I felt that the language could be modernized without loss and that the resultant improvement in clarity would be worth the effort. My understanding of musical structures and my ability to sing in tune have both improved in the process.

Daniel Rivers-Moore
August 1994

La novità del suono e il grande lume
di lor cagion m'accesero un disío
mai non sentito di cotanto acume. . . .
Tu non séi in terra sì come tu credi; . . .
"Qui veggion l'alte creature l'orma
dell'etterno valore, il quale è fine,
al quale è fatta la toccata norma."

(Dante, Paradiso 1.82-108)

The newness of the sound,
And that great light, inflamed me with desire,
Keener than e'er was felt, to know their cause. . . .
Thou art not on the earth as thou believest; . . .
(Then said Beatrice) "Here
The higher creatures see the printed steps
Of that eternal power, which is the end
For which the order of things is made."

(Cary's translation, adapted)

Chapter One

METAPHYSICAL CORRESPONDENCES

All music is based on the relations between sounds, and a careful study of the numbers by which these relations are ruled brings us immediately into the almost forgotten science of numerical symbolism. Numbers correspond to abstract principles, and their application to physical reality follows absolute and inescapable laws. In musical experience we are brought into direct contact with these principles; the connection between physical reality and metaphysical principles can be felt in music as nowhere else. Music was therefore justly considered by the ancients as the key to all sciences and arts—the link between metaphysics and physics through which the universal laws and their multiple applications could be understood.

Modern civilization has tended to reject the ways of thinking and scientific conceptions that formed its foundations. Western people have largely broken away from the social and intellectual regulations that restricted their freedom, and in doing so they have abandoned the age-old order and traditional knowledge that had been the basis of their development. This is why sciences and arts originally understood as diverse applications of common principles have been reduced to a condition of fragmentary experiments isolated from one another.

Thus, to take the domain with which we are here particularly concerned, there remain no data in the West on the nature of music except for a few technical and mostly arbitrary rules about the relations of sounds and the structures of chords. The strange phenomenon by which coordinated sounds have the power to evoke feelings or images is accepted simply as a fact. Attempts are made to define the effects of certain combinations of sounds, but these effects are discovered almost fortuitously and no search is made for their underlying cause. Just as one day Newton discovered the law of gravitation, it is only through the genius of some musician that we may be able to rediscover the significance of a particular relation of sounds; it is Gluck or Chopin who may suddenly reveal to us the deep, absolute, and inevitable meaning of a chord or of a melodic interval.

Unfortunately, such fragmentary experiments do not allow us to reconstruct the general laws that would give us the key to all foreseen and unforeseen combinations, and these experimental discoveries remain without any logical connection.

The idea that all sciences are ultimately experimental is so dear to Westerners that they do not even notice that all the elements of their musical system are symbolic—as are almost all their ways of measuring time and space as well—and that if those elements appear to us as *natural*, it is only because of the correspondence between the symbols and the perceptible world. We find in supposedly scientific writings the poetic story of the primitive human who, having cut a bamboo stalk and blown through it, discovers the diatonic scale as defined by Zarlino, which is supposed to be the "natural scale." Such myths simply show their authors' complete ignorance of the thousands of scales that are possible, expressive, pleasant to the ear, and perfectly natural and legitimate.

Besides, the real problem is not to know how human beings may have acquired the knowledge of musical intervals, which always brings us back to a question of myth, ancient or modern, but to find out the real nature of the phenomenon by which some sounds can be combined to represent ideas, images, or feelings. This we obviously cannot discover by experiment nor decide by vote. So we shall have to draw upon the data of traditional metaphysics; though it may take many forms at different times and in different places, metaphysics always presents the same logical and coherent structure, of which we shall presently try to give an outline.

"All things," Dante once wrote, "are arranged in a certain order, and this order constitutes the form by which the universe resembles God."[1] If sounds can evoke in us emotions, beings, or landscapes, it is because there are correspondences between different aspects of the manifested world that the laws of music allow us to bring out.

In the *Li ji* (Book of Rites), edited by Confucius, we read that "music is intimately connected with the essential relations between beings"; and, according to Dong Zhongzu (second century B.C.E.):

> The vital spirits of humankind, tuned to the tone of heaven and earth, express all the tremors of heaven and earth, just as several cithars, all tuned on *gong* [tonic], all vibrate when the note *gong* sounds. The fact of harmony between heaven and earth and humankind does not come from a physical union, from a direct action; it comes from a tuning on the same note producing vibrations in unison. . . . In the universe nothing happens by chance, there is no spontaneity; all is influence and harmony, accord answering accord.[2]

To be able to realize the nature of this accord between the different aspects of the universe, we must know the principles that are common to all these aspects. This is why theorists of Indian music assert that although subtle correspondences can be experimentally discovered between the laws of nature and the laws of harmony, between the modes of music and the modes of our feelings, they can be completely and logically explained only by traditional metaphysics, whose source is in the Vedas. As René Guénon explains:

> The affirmation of the perpetuity of the Vedas is directly connected with the cosmological theory of the primordial nature of sound among sensible qualities (sound being the particular quality of ether, *ākāśa*, which is the first element). And this theory is in reality nothing other than that which is expressed in other traditions when 'creation by the Word' is spoken of. The primordial sound is the divine Word, through which, according to the first chapter of the Hebrew Genesis, all things were made. This is why it is said that the *Rishis* or sages of the first ages 'heard' the Vedas. Revelation, being a work of the Word like creation itself, is actually a hearing for those who receive it.[3]

According to Kśemarāja:

> The *bindu*, wanting to manifest the thought it has of all things, vibrates, and is transformed into a [primordial] sound with the nature of a cry [*nāda*]. It shouts out the universe, which is not distinct from itself; that is to say, it thinks it—hence the word *śabda* [word]. Meditation is the supreme 'word': it sounds, that is, it vibrates, submitting all things to the fragmentation of life; this is why it is *nāda* [vibration]. . . . Sound [*śabda*], which is of the nature of *nāda*, resides in all living beings.[4]

Swāmi Hariharānand Saraswatī explained the fundamental interdependence of sounds and forms as follows:

> The *things named* and their *names* are parallel manifestations resulting from the union of *Brahman* [undifferentiated principle] and *Māyā* [appearances] just as waves appear in the sea. From *Brahman* united with *Sakti* [Energy = *Māyā*] issue, in the order of manifestation of the world, on the one hand the *principle of naming*, from it the monosyllable *Om*, and from *Om* all words [or sounds], and on the other hand, the *principle of forms* and out of it all the world, living beings, etc. But between those two aspects of manifestation, the relation remains close; there is fundamental identity between the principle of names and the principle of forms, as well as between words and objects.[5]

The universe is called in Sanskrit *jagat* (that which moves) because nothing exists but by the combination of forces and movements. But every movement generates a vibration and therefore a *sound* that is peculiar to it. Such a sound, of course, may not be audible to our rudimentary ears, but it does exist as pure sound. Since each element of matter produces a sound, the relation of elements can be expressed by a relation of sounds. We can therefore understand why astrology, alchemy, geometry, and so forth express themselves in terms of harmonic relations.

Although those pure, absolute sounds that Kabir calls "inaudible music" cannot be perceived by our ears (they may be perceptible for more delicate instruments, and the perception of such sounds is one of the stages in the practice of yoga), we may nonetheless be able to produce corresponding sounds within the range of vibrations we can perceive. We can establish relations between these partial sounds similar to the subtle relations of nature. They will be only gross relations, but they may approach the subtle relations of nature sufficiently to evoke images in our mind. Sir John Woodroffe, the learned commentator on tantric metaphysics, explains it thus: "There are, it is said, closely approximate natural names, combined according to natural laws of harmony [*chandahs*], forming *mantras* which are irresistibly connected with their esoteric *arthas* [forms]."[6]

If we were able to reproduce the exact relations that constitute the natural names, we should recreate beings, things, and phenomena, because this is the very process of creation, explained by the Vedas and also indicated in Genesis, or in the Gospel of John when the "creative Word" is spoken of. If, however, exact relations cannot be produced, approximate relations have a power, if not of creation, at least of evocation; sound "works now in man's small magic, just as it first worked in the grand magical display of the World Creator."[7] "The natural name of anything is the sound which is produced by the action of the moving forces which constitute it. He therefore, it is said, who mentally or vocally utters with creative force the natural name of anything brings into being the thing which bears that name."[8] By the artificial construction of harmony we can go beyond the phenomenon of sound vibrations and perceive not sounds but immaterial relations through which can be expressed realities of a spiritual nature. We can thus lift the veil by which matter hides from us all true realities.

By "the mutual aiding and inhibiting of the sounds in the *Chhandas*[9] collocation . . . the cumulative effect of the repetition of sounds and strings of sounds also may produce the aforesaid result."[10] The effect produced by a group of sounds is practically the same whether their collocation is simultaneous (chords) or successive (modes), the numerical relation being identical in the two cases.

Evocation through sound, like creation itself, takes place not because of the material fact of physical vibration but on account of the existence of metaphysical correspondences. Therefore all psychological explanation of musical experience has to be discarded. In reality, the personality of the hearer counts for nothing in the phenomenon of musical evocation because evocation takes place even if there is no hearer, and if the existence of this evocation is ephemeral it is only because of the imperfection of the relation of sounds. Hearers can be differentiated negatively only by the relative acuteness of their perceptions, their greater or lesser deafness.

"Several centuries before Plato, Pythagoras, imbued with Egyptian doctrine, requested his disciples to reject the judgment of their ears as susceptible to error and variation where harmonic principles are concerned. He wanted them to regulate those immovable principles only according to the proportional and analogical harmony of numbers."[11] The work of the musician consists therefore only in knowing, as accurately as possible, the symbolic relations of all things so as to reproduce in us, through the magic of sounds, the feelings, the passions, the visions of an almost real world. And the history of Indian music, as that of Chinese music, is full of the legends of marvelous musicians whose voice could make night fall or spring appear, or who, like the celebrated musician Naik Gopal, compelled by the Emperor Akbar to sing in the mode of fire (*rāga Dīpak*), made the water of the river Jumna boil and died burned by the flames that issued from every part of his body.

The ancient Greeks, too, knew the science of connections between sounds and other aspects of manifestation, a science that for modern Westerners goes under the name of magic. "Everything obeys a secret music of which the *Tetractys* is the numerical symbol, and the man who, like the initiated Pythagorean, has understood its true laws can achieve apparent miracles. It is, for example, with the sounds of the lyre that Amphion built the walls of Thebes."[12] The mathematical laws of music are part of the laws by which the world's harmony is regulated. This is why we shall find in music the same characteristics, the same geometry, the same particular numbers that are found in other aspects of the universe.

Michael Maier, the seventeenth-century hermeticist and physician, attempted to determine these relations:

> Like all visible things that are in nature, celestial bodies as well as terrestrial ones have been created in terms of number, weight, and measure. There is thus between them an admirable and marvelous proportion in the parts, the forces, the qualities, the quantities, and their effects, from which results a very harmonious music. There is also a kind of accord and musical concert between spiritual beings, among which the soul and the human intellect are included.
>
> In the great system of this universe there is a *ditone* [third] from the earth, which is the base, to the sphere of the moon; from there up to the sun, which is the heart, a *diapente* [fifth]; and from the sun to the supreme heaven a *diapason* [octave]; so that the first distance is composed of eigh-

teen commas or intervals, the second of thirty-six, and the third of sixty-one.[13] In the microcosm or little world, that is to say in man, one can see a similar proportion between the main parts, which are the liver, the heart, and the brain, counting from the soles of the feet, not as mathematicians or geometers do, but as physicists do.[14]

To be able to establish the correspondence between sounds and the different aspects of the universe, we must divide the indefinite progression of sound according to certain proportions, which are determined by the cyclic character of certain intervals and the properties of fundamental numbers.

According to the formula of the Tao-te ching , "One has given birth to two, two has given birth to three, three has given birth to all numbers."[15] In musical terms this principle manifests itself as the original sound first producing its octave (a frequency ratio of 2/1) giving duality, then a third sound, the fifth (3/2), from which all other sounds are born. Among these sounds, in indefinite number, we must select a few whose respective ratios are adequate for the representation of the world in which we are living. In this way the scale of sounds has been formed, corresponding to the material world, to the five directions of space (four cardinal directions and the center), the five elements, and so on. This is the basis on which develops the whole system of the harmony of fifths, which through their cycles form first a series of twelve sounds, then a series of fifty-two sounds, and finally a series of sixty sounds within the octave. As explained in an extremely ancient Chinese treatise, "the five degrees, born from the principles yin and yang, divide themselves into the twelve lü which, by their revolutions, produce the sixty lü."[16]

To these five principal sounds are added two auxiliary ones to form the scale of seven notes, the image of the celestial world, which corresponds with the seven visible planets in the world of spheres. Plato, in his Timaeus, noted that the soul of the world is divided into seven parts. And this is why it was the seven-stringed lyre that symbolized the beauty or the harmony of the spheres. Each string of the lyre was related to a planet. The musical sounds themselves were given the names of planets, and "because the mathematical laws observed in musical art and in cosmic spheres are related to the natural rhythms of the soul,"[17] music forms a logical and direct tie between the movements of the world and the movements of our soul.

The steps by which Dante rose up to the supreme light also numbered seven: "the imprinted steps of the eternal power, which is the end for which the order of things is made."[18] "But what are these steps? They are precisely the different aspects assumed by this eternal power on which the order of the universe rests; they are the seven differentiations of the one light, the seven colors of the prism and of the rainbow, the seven sounds contained in the primordial sound, the seven luminaries by which is reflected onto our Earth the light of the eternal great luminary that shines in the center of this vastness."[19] They are the seven horses that drag the chariot of Sūrya, the Hindu sun god. The union of the ternary and the quaternary, the sevenfold (4 + 3) symbol of the soul of the world, was represented by the seven pipes of the flute of Pan, the god of the universe.

Assimilated to the seven planets, the seven notes move across the twelve regions of the octave, corresponding to the signs of the zodiac, in which, as we shall see later, these seven notes will occupy twenty-two main positions (a number that is in certain cases reduced to seventeen). We shall also see why the twelve regions of the octave cannot be assimilated to twelve fixed sounds, as has been attempted in the tempered scale. They determine the space in which the notes move but can in no way be taken for the notes themselves:

> The number twelve, formed by the combination of the ternary and the quaternary ($3 \times 4 = 12$),[20] is the symbol of the universe and the measure of sounds. . . . Pythagoras, Timaeus of Locres, and Plato, when they gave the dodecahedron as the symbol of the universe, only restated the ideas of the Egyptians, the Chaldeans, the Greeks. . . . The institution of the zodiac is the result of the application of the number twelve to the supreme sphere. . . . The number twelve, so applied to the universe and all its representations, was always the harmonic manifestation of the principles One and Two and of the way in which their elements were coordinated. It was therefore also the symbol of the coordination of sounds and, as such, applied to the lyre of Hermes.[21]

Built on such bases, music becomes a difficult science capable of a profound action. "In ancient times, music was something other than mere pleasure of the ear: it was like an algebra of metaphysical abstractions, knowledge of which was given only to initiates, but by whose principles the masses were instinctively and unconsciously influenced. This is what made music one of the most powerful instruments of moral education, as Confucious had said before Plato."[22]

But there is an imperfection at the very basis of the world's existence, because if the world were perfect it would immediately be reabsorbed into the infinite perfection. The heart is not in the center of the chest, the axis of the earth is oblique, and the solar year does not coincide with the lunar year (thus creating the cycles by which all existence is conditioned and human destinies measured). In the same way the development of twelve fifths, instead of bringing us back precisely to the octave, leaves a difference—the comma—with which we shall have to negotiate. This will complicate every calculation and prevent us from formulating those rigid and simple laws, attractive but inaccurate, in which our vain reason delights. This comma, which the modern world tries so hard to ignore, represents, for those who can understand it, the essential difference between what is finite and what is infinite. The fifths form a spiral whose sounds, coiled around themselves, can never meet. For us, this limitless spiral can be the joint in the structure of the world, the narrow gate that will allow us to escape from the appearance of a closed universe, to travel in other worlds and explore their secrets.

Only by respecting such subtle differences can the edifice of sounds become the image of reality and one of the ways of spiritual realization. "It is literally by way of 'assonance,' of 'accord,' that he who 'understands' [*evamvit*] is assimilated to the source of light or (in Christian terminology) assumes a glorified body. . . . And this is possible precisely because, as Plotinus expresses it, this music is 'a terrestrial representation of the music that exists in the kingdom of the ideal world.'"[23]

Even if we leave aside the role of music as a means of spiritual realization, the effect of musical chords and modes (*rāgas*) is much more far-reaching than our ears are at first able to allow us to perceive. Our ears can apparently be satisfied by a very approximate accuracy. Yet a perfectly accurate interval not only acts on our ears but also produces a transformation in all the cells of our body—a slowing down or an acceleration in the movements of every molecule in ourselves and in the surrounding matter. This effect was used to cure certain diseases, not only in India but also in ancient Greece and later in Persia and Arabia. Muhammad Hafid describes at length these musical therapies, indicating the scale to employ for each disease. But if we habitually use inaccurate intervals on the grounds that our ear does not clearly perceive the difference, the effect that those sounds will produce on our organism can well be the opposite of that which our complacent ears persist in accepting. It is with our mind alone that we accept this inaccurate music, which leaves us tired and tense through an unconscious effort of adaptation, instead of agreeably transformed by the beneficial influence of the harmony.

This is why disregarding small differences in intervals has very grave consequences with regard to the deeper effect of music, consequences that can only be neglected when the real purpose of art is totally misunderstood. Unfortunately the materialistic and highly utilitarian tendencies of our times rarely allow people to bother about anything that is not immediately tangible. We daily use all sorts of forces, recently domesticated, in total ignorance of their effect on the structure of our organism and on the balance of external events. This is why we find it quite normal to change the course of sounds if to do so brings some immediate simplification; and this leads us to try to change the endless spiral of fifths into a closed circle, to tear up the comma and divide it between the other notes and so bring the cycle of sounds within the narrow limits of human logic. Whatever advantages may be obtained by such an action (and there is no doubt that such advantages do exist), we nevertheless expel the heavenly element from music when we obliterate the possibilities of contacts with spiritual forces by disfiguring the intervals. When music is thus reformed it loses its true purpose, and its magical effects, henceforth uncontrolled, can become dangerous. It is not without reason that Plato has Damo, the last of the great Pythagorean teachers, declare that "one cannot touch the musical modes without disrupting the constitution of the state."[24] He could as well have said "without disregarding universal order."

As René Guénon says,

> In ancient times, as can be seen particularly clearly in the Far East, modifications could be brought into music only in accordance with changes that had occurred in the very conditions of the world, according to cyclic periods. This is because musical rhythms were intimately related both to the human and social order and to the cosmic order, and even in some way expressed the relation between the two. The Pythagorean theory of the 'harmony of the spheres' is connected with exactly the same sort of consideration.[25]

For the world to be in a state of equilibrium, its different elements need to be harmonized. Since music expresses the relations between human and cosmic orders, it must respect the exact intervals on which these relations are based, as determined by the traditional data that define those relations. Disregard for such an obvious law necessarily leads to a breakdown of equilibrium and social disorder, as the *Yue ji* declares:

> If the *gong* [tonic: C (Sa)[26]] is disturbed, then there is disorganization: the prince is arrogant.
>
> If the *shang* [tonic: D (Re)] is disturbed, then there is deviation: the officials are corrupted.
>
> If the *jiao* [tonic: E (Ga)] is disturbed, then there is anxiety: the people are unhappy.
>
> If the *zhi* [tonic: G (Pa)] is disturbed, then there is complaint: public services are too heavy.
>
> If the *yu* [tonic: A+ (Dha+)] is disturbed, then there is danger: resources are lacking.
>
> If the five degrees are all disturbed, then there is danger: ranks encroach upon each other (this is what is called impudence) and, if such is the condition, the destruction of the kingdom may come in less than a day. . . .
>
> In periods of disorder, rites are altered and music is licentious. Then sad sounds are lacking in dignity, joyful sounds lacking in calmness. . . . When the spirit of opposition manifests itself, indecent music comes into being. . . . when the spirit of conformity manifests itself, harmonious music appears. . . . So, under the effect of music, the five social duties are without admixture, the eyes and the ears are clear, the blood and the vital spirits are balanced, habits are reformed, customs are improved, the empire is in complete peace.[27]

~ *Chapter Two* ~

TH£ (ONF£LICT
OF MUSICAL SYSTEMS

The Different Musical Systems

Western musicians have a tendency to believe that their musical theory and notation are sufficient to express everything. When they hear of other intervals, they think of quarter tones, commas, and other small units, which in their opinion may have curiosity value but no serious importance so far as the general structure of music is concerned. Yet we can observe the total inability of the Western system and notation to render the melodies and chords of Asian music without completely disfiguring them.

We might be tempted to conclude, as has often been suggested, that Eastern peoples have a different theory and are using different intervals from those of Westerners. But a more serious study shows us that these apparently different intervals all have as their basis the same definitions and refer to the same acoustic principles. Hence the difference can only come either from a musical practice in contradiction to theory, or from the use of only some of the possibilities opened up by those common principles. We shall see that both these causes must be considered.

As noted by Raouf Yekta Bey, "Music, like the other mathematical sciences, is a science whose laws are fixed and invariable. Just as two and two make four in the East as well as in the West, the fundamental laws of music apply at all times and for all peoples. The differences in view which can be noted among theorists in each century and in each country can originate only from their greater or lesser lack of insight into the many questions whose study requires a theoretical and practical knowledge of music."[1]

The musical system actually employed in the West is far from being a logical and absolute system based on irrefutable acoustic realities. It is the result of a mixture of traditions that has been arbitrarily simplified without taking into account, or without the knowledge of, the principles on which the component systems were based. Because so simplified a musical system was insufficient, musicians have attempted to develop a kind of "dictionary of harmonic relations" according to their observations or their instinct, accumulating many discoveries and observations, but without any explanation of their cause or the reason for their significance.

These different musical systems do not oppose one another. On the contrary, they complete each other, as they all spring necessarily from the same fundamental laws of which they exploit different aspects. Like the forms of language, musical modes are permanent marks of the tradition to which a people belongs. Wherever artificial systems have not destroyed or disfigured traditional musical modes, it is as easy by the study of music as by that of linguistics to observe the migrations of races and their influences upon each other. Striking examples are the importation of Mongolian scales into China by Genghis Khan or that of Persian modes into Northern India. In the West, in spite of the havoc created by the tempered scale, it is quite easy to find the continuity of Celtic modes from Scotland to North Africa, while the modes of Spanish gypsies are actually Indian modes, even in minute details of execution.

But before we can study musical systems, it is necessary to define the exact nature of sounds and their relations.

The Structure of Musical Sounds

Any object made to vibrate produces a combination of sound waves that, depending on its composition, is more or less pleasant to the ear and more or less "musical." This sound is formed of one or more fundamental notes and other notes called harmonics. The sounds used in music generally have only one fundamental note. The harmonics of this fundamental, according to their relative intensity, give the sound its characteristic timbre or color, making it appear more or less pure or more or less nasal (the harmonics of a flute, for example, are weak, while those of a violin are much stronger). When with the help of different instruments some of these harmonics are reinforced, the quality of the basic sound is enhanced, and its expressive value, which differs according to the specific harmonics reinforced, is improved. Thus is born harmony, which is the art of superimposing sounds. If the sounds are successive rather than simultaneous, the notion of time intervenes and we have to call upon memory to establish the harmonic relations, which alone give melody its meaning.

The group of two or three fundamental chords that contain all the notes of a melody is called a mode. The relations between the notes that constitute a mode can be represented numerically. The mode is then, with its complete significance, represented by a group of numerical relations. Chords can be represented in the same way.

In the musical systems in which the tonic is permanent and constantly present to the mind of the listener, each note has a significance determined by its relation to the tonic. The melody is thus composed of a succession of sounds with a perfectly definite meaning, and therefore its significance is absolutely clear. But if the tonic is not absolutely permanent, no note can have a significance unless the ratio that measures its expression is also given. This is why, in every musical system where modulation (or change of tonic) is admitted, it can be asserted that no note and no melody can have a significance without the harmonic context, which alone establishes the ratios necessary to define the meaning of each note and consequently of the entire melody.

The mode, being a series of sounds that have definite relations to a permanent tonic, can truly be said to represent the fixed harmonic basis of all melodic music, modulation being almost unknown in modal music, as the harmonic uncertainty it would create would last too long. The melodic figures, turning within a fixed circle and coming back frequently to certain notes, create a harmonic complex that gives its significance to the melody.

Gounod once wrote, "Sounds alone can no more constitute music than words alone can constitute a language. Words can only form a proposition, an intelligible sentence, when they are associated in a logical sequence according to the laws of intellect. This is also true of sounds, whose production, successive or simultaneous, must obey certain laws of attraction and mutual response before they can become a musical reality, a musical thought."[2]

Relations between Sounds

The number of possible musical intervals is obviously unlimited in theory. But because of the limits of discrimination of our ears and the consonant properties of some ratios, the number of intervals used in musical practice is limited. Things are different in magic, where the absolute precision of a mathematical interval is necessary to produce the desired phenomenon, but for a musical evocation, the simpler acoustic intervals are sufficient. Besides, they appear so natural that without external help it is vocally almost impossible to get away from them, "the sounds that form consonances being the only ones that the human ear can accurately detect and the human vocal organ spontaneously utter."[3]

If in musical practice only a small number of intervals can be used that have definite ratios between them, it must be possible to devise a scale that allows all possible combinations of such ratios. To determine such a scale we must attempt to discover the laws of numbers on which such a division must necessarily be based, and we must study the methods used in the application of these laws to musical practice by different peoples at different periods. Then, comparing the structures of the most important systems, we shall see whether it is possible to bring all the intervals that they use within a single framework without distorting them as equal temperament does.

For our investigation, musical intervals appear under two aspects: one mathematical, involving numbers and logical ratios; the other symbolic and psychological, in which the relations of sounds (their harmony) awaken in us feelings, ideas, and precise visions. These two aspects obviously have their origin in the same principles, but this unity is beyond the scope of experiment and consequently beyond the understanding of modern Westerners. This deficiency naturally brings them to the illogical situation of leaving aside one aspect of experience whenever they study the other, as if the laws of acoustics and those of musical expression did not refer to the same sounds.

Fifth and Octave

According to circumstances, time, and the role attributed to music, theorists have compiled musical theories from the point of view of either expression or numbers. We shall see that in the first case, the basis is generally the interval of the octave and the relations of the notes to a fixed sound—the tonic. This gives birth to modal music. In the second case, emphasis is given to the properties of the interval of the fifth, and the successions of fifths, which leads to modulation and therefore to harmony.

"The conflict of the fifth and the octave, the impossibility of going from one to the other, could not escape the notice of musicians and theorists. . . . This difficulty, known to Jiao Yanshou and Jing Fang, led them to the [division of the octave into] sixty *lü*, which they explained by comparisons with natural philosophy."[4]

Obviously, in the beginning such an opposition did not exist because, as all the traditions assert, people still looked at things from the metaphysical point of view, which explains this apparent dualism. Unfortunately, even in Indian tradition, the definitions that have reached us on such fundamental points are often fragmentary and intentionally obscure. But such definitions are implied by the very text of certain sacred books, and a deeper study of such books can always provide a key to those who are able to understand and interpret them.

Octave and Mode

In modal music, intervals are measured by the relation of the different notes to the tonic (Sa). The numbers that symbolize those relations form ratios that are generally simple and allow comparisons to be made, for instance, between musical harmony and the proportions of sacred architecture, the proportions of the human body, the relations of colors, the divisions of time, and so forth. Furthermore, aesthetic emotion being the mark of the correspondence of our subtle self with certain ratios, we can with the help of those ratios determine the fundamental numbers on which the human organism is based. These common proportions constitute the key whereby we can understand the real structure of music and unlock its power. They determine the significance of chords taken individually, as well as that of the systems of modal music, whether Indian, Turkish, or Arabic. They also determine the modes used by ancient Greek musicians, though these must be distinguished from the modes defined by the Greek physicists, which are based on a different principle.

The relations to the tonic are brought out in modal music by the almost continuous sounding of the tonic. This constant tonic is called *ison* in Byzantine music (*Shadja*, or *Sa*, in modern Indian music). It seems that modern Westerners are completely unable to perceive these relations with the tonic. The remarks of Bourgault-Ducoudray comparing the *ison* to a spit piercing through the melody, or of Amédée Gastoué saying, "It is not, as far as we know, because of a need for harmony that the *ison* was introduced [*sic*] into Byzantine chant, but because of the need to keep the singers in tune,"[5] imply that they have not the slightest idea of those relations that are, properly speaking, the harmony of so-called monodic music and outside of which melody has little effect or meaning. It would be just as ridiculous to speak of *adding* a fundamental to a chord, since a chord exists only in relation to its fundamental note.

The *ison* or "equal" of Byzantine music was called *chandovatī śruti* (the measuring sound) in ancient Indian music. It is, properly speaking, the standard by which all intervals are measured. No interval, no note, no melody has a meaning unless the *ison* (Sa) is present. It seems that Westerners are just as unable to "hear" these relations as Easterners are to perceive chords, but this is not a sufficient reason to consider either system unpleasant and useless. The *ison* defines the meaning of each note, which can be expressed by a numerical ratio, exactly as harmony does. And melody without *ison* is just as flavorless as is, for the modern Westerner, melody without harmony. When they disregard the importance of the *ison*, learned and respectable Westerners only show that they understand nothing of the Eastern music they pretend to study and explain, and that they perceive nothing of its marvelous power.

The *mesa* was, to ancient Greek music, what the *ison* is to modern Byzantine music. "For the ancient [Greeks], the A (*mesa*) is a directional string whose *permanent* use constitutes a guiding mark for the ear and a reduction to unity for the mind."[6] The *mesa* is "the connecting element of successive sounds . . . the connecting agent of all the melodic forms of the octave."[7]

Eastern listeners often make such remarks as "The Beethoven symphonies are very interesting, but why have all those chords been introduced, spoiling the charm of the melodies?" From such responses we can know for certain that they do not perceive the essential elements of the music. Their failure to understand is similar to that of the Westerner who refuses to admit that modal music has a full musical significance without the addition of harmony.

Such misunderstandings are not without serious consequences. To realize this, it is sufficient to hear so-called Oriental melodies *arranged* by Western composers, or, still better, to hear the so-called Westernized orchestras that graced the courts of many Indian *rājas* during the first half of this century, where "harmony" was understood to be the art of playing together as many disconnected sounds as possible.

In modal music, the pedal point of the tonic is indispensable for the melody to have its expressions because other notes, when they are accentuated, would have a tendency to substitute themselves for the tonic and so render the expression of the mode completely indeterminate.

Suppose, for example, using the diatonic scale (the white keys of the piano), we choose the mode of A (Dha) (*rāga Yavanpurī Todī*), whose third, sixth, and seventh degrees are minor. If we do not maintain the pedal point of the tonic A (Dha), then C (Sa) will have a tendency to become the tonic instead of the minor third. The meaning of every note will be changed and, since the modes will destroy each other, melodies will be without expression, as is the case with Western melody if it is not harmonized.

It is the loss of this tonic pedal somewhere in the course of history that renders the modes of plainchant so vague and so weak. They lack a basis, and so their classification becomes a rather abstract game, like the system of the Greek *Doristi* in the unreal form generally attributed to it. It is only by an artificial conception that a mode can be assimilated to the plagal[8] form of another mode. It is not sufficient to state that D (Re), E (Ga), or G (Pa) has been chosen as a tonic to obtain the corresponding mode in any melody. The melody remains unaffected and in the key of C (Sa) because a permanent element is required to determine a key and habit can up to a point create this permanence in favor of C (Sa)—that is, in favor of the Western major mode, supposing that we are still using only the white notes of the piano keyboard. Another mode can be created only by constantly imposing its tonic. Percussion instruments, such as drums or cymbals, can be sufficient to determine this tonic. This is why the problem did not arise in ancient music, as such instruments were always present in a musical performance. The accurate tuning of the different notes of the scale should, of course, be sufficient to define the tonic, but as the differences between the intervals are very small, rare indeed are the musicians who can maintain this accuracy without referring constantly to the tonic.

Fifth and Modulation

In modal music, as soon as the tonic moves, the modal structure crumbles and every note loses its former significance. But in connection with the changing cycle of fifths, some new permanent relations can be established, and those relations will evoke other aspects of the universal structure. In the cycle of fifths we can perceive the reflection of the world of spheres in which we dwell. We shall find in it the laws that regulate the movements of planets, those of seasons and of days, and all those cycles that, within this universe, measure our destinies.[9]

Starting from a given point—the general tonic—the fifths will form ratios at first simple but becoming more and more complicated. If we take as a basis the note adapted to the cosmic period, the year, the month, and the day, these ratios will allow us to find out auspicious days for events both past and future. This is the traditional system of the Chinese, and its use in official ceremonies, as we noted already in the *Yue ji*, helped to maintain order, political harmony, and security within the empire. But it can also contribute to their overthrow because it is the inescapable instrument of magical achievements.

Still, every system exclusively based on the properties of fifths remains incomplete from certain points of view. Fabre d'Olivet says that such a system "will always lack the descending chromatic and enharmonic. Rameau, who, more than eight thousand years after Ling Lun, wanted to make it the basis of his musical system, starting from the same experiment, was forced to resort to an insipid temperament that mutilates every sound and that, proposed twenty times in China, was twenty times rejected because the scholars of the nation, although they had known for a long time the hollowness of their system, preferred to keep it pure, if incomplete, rather than spoil it in one of its parts in order to make up for what was missing."[10]

Harmony and Temperament

Following the mistake of the ancient Greeks, the European classical system is divided between the two antagonistic tendencies of mode and modulation. Although built without any "scientific" method, using aspects of each system, it has given rise to some remarkable developments by taking advantage of this lack of a rational theory. The importance of these developments in the general history of music should not be overestimated, however. By allowing such aberrations as equal temperament, the lack of a proper theoretical foundation will in all probability quickly drive the European classical system to complete decadence. The success of African American music, with its "blue" notes so alien to equal temperament and therefore so expressive, is not due merely to fashion. It shows the need for an understandable musical system, for logical and true intervals that can remove the veil of inexpressive insipidity which temperament spreads over even the most impassioned movements of the greatest symphonies.

Melodic Expression or Harmonic Expression

The development of harmony corresponds in modern Western music to a parallel destruction of modes. From the strict point of view of musical expression, that is, from the amount of feeling and wealth of imagery that the music is able to convey, it is thus very difficult to assert that the harmonic system gives greater possibilities of expression than any modal system. The means of expression differ but the possibilities seem equal.

Many imagine that it would be best to combine both systems, as has often been attempted. But this is not possible because of the almost complete opposition between them. Except for a few fundamental chords, which are also used in modal music as ornaments, all chord changes and modulations are made possible only by violating the fine distinctions in the structure of the intervals that are at the very root of modal expression.

"It is therefore the introduction of harmony in musical art that has caused the disappearance of the distinction between the ancient modes. It is because of this . . . that our musical system is limited to the only two modes that possess a distinctive harmony and completely different chords: the major and minor modes, which are . . . those in which the greatest simplicity is united with the greatest number of differences."[11]

All those who have been in contact with ancient Western modal music, or with the music of the Middle and Far East, have deplored the ruin of melody and rhythm that accompanies the development of harmony, a phenomenon that could be observed throughout the nineteenth century and that is still observable in such northern countries as Russia, Scotland, and Ireland.

N. A. Willard has even said (not without foundation) that "modern melody has not the merit of the ancient and . . . [thus] harmony is used with the view of compensating for its poorness and diverting the attention of the audience from perceiving the barrenness of genius."[12] No better description could be given of a great number of modern works.

Jean-Jacques Rousseau once remarked,

> If we bear in mind that of all the people of the earth, who all possess music and songs, Europeans are the only ones who use harmony and chords and find this mixture pleasant; if we bear in mind that, of all the nations who cultivated fine arts, not one used this harmony;[13] that no animal, no bird, no being in nature produces any other sound than unison, any other music than melody; that Oriental languages, so sonorous and so musical, that Greek ears, so delicate, so sensitive, trained with so much art, have never guided those voluptuous and passionate peoples toward our harmony; that their music had such extraordinary effects; that ours has such feeble ones; that, finally, it was to be the privilege of northern races, whose hard and rough organs are more impressed by the shrillness and the noise of voices than by the softness of accents and the melody of inflections, to make this great discovery and to put it forward as the principle of all the rules of art; if, I say, we bear all this in mind, it is very difficult not to suspect that all our harmony is only a gothic and barbarous invention, to which we would never have taken had we been more sensitive to the real beauty of art and of truly natural music.[14]

Of course, modern people, who accept so seriously many another of Rousseau's theories, which are much more difficult to demonstrate, smile at such rhetoric, but they would have great difficulty in contradicting it. As Fabre d'Olivet has very justly remarked, "It is true that our modern symphonists, who can understand nothing of the marvels described by the ancients, prefer to deny them. But a denial is not an answer, and it is not sufficient to say that something is untrue for it to be so."[15]

Famous Western scholars have spoken with irony of such irrational conceptions. Sir William Jones once wrote, "The astonishing effects ascribed to music by the old *Greeks* and, in our days, by the *Chinese, Persians* and *Indians,* have probably been exaggerated and embellished; nor, if such effects had been really produced, could they be imputed, I think, to the mere influence of sounds, however combined and modified."[16] Happily, Jones lets us know what sort of effects he attributes to music in terms that show quite clearly the understanding he has of the subject: "After food, when the operations of digestion and absorption give so much employment to the vessels that a temporary state of mental repose must be found, especially in hot climates, essential to health, it seems reasonable to believe that a few agreeable airs, either heard or played without effort, must have all the good effect of sleep and none of its disadvantages; *putting* the soul in tune, as Milton, says."[17]

It is only natural that the followers of a particular musical system, as those of a particular religion, should consider the followers of another school with contempt. This only proves that they have that absolute faith in the path they follow without which no realization is possible. But if we want to rise above mere practice and search for the principles that allow such realizations, we have to give up the outlook of faith and accept only the logic of reason. We shall then observe that, although we are at first utterly unable to discern in a strange form of music anything comparable to what we experience directly and without effort in a form familiar to us, an impartial scrutiny will show that all the essential elements or relations that are found in the one are also present in the other. There is, consequently, no theoretical reason why the same expressions, the same realizations, should not be equally possible through these different forms.

Therefore, in judging the possibilities and the value of musical systems, we should not trust the prejudiced judgment of our ears, but consider in their most abstract form their theoretical possibilities. We may then discover the equivalence of systems that at first seem to have nothing in common. We may also discover a profound difference between systems whose forms are outwardly very similar. By so doing we shall, in any case, judge the musical systems soundly and on safe grounds. To be able to realize their beauty or directly perceive their meaning is another matter and generally requires very long practice.

Chapter Three

THE MEASUREMENT
OF INTERVALS
AND HARMONIC SOUNDS

*There are two effects, one seen and one unseen. Svaras
[notes] when thrown here and there without order cannot
produce any results. Therefore, to realize all results, seen
and unseen, we shall define* grāma *[scale] first.*

Saṅgīta Ratnākara

Measurement of Intervals

To be in a position to study different musical systems, we must first look at the
methods of measuring musical intervals and decide which method we shall use.

On any stringed instrument, to obtain equal intervals at different pitches,
we have to use smaller differences in string length the higher we go in the scale.
This is because the frequency of the note produced is inversely proportional to
the length of the string, and equal intervals correspond to a geometrical progression of frequencies.

To define a musical interval, the simplest system is of course either to note
the ratio of the string lengths or pipe lengths that produce the notes, which is
the ancient system, or to note the ratio of the frequencies of the notes (which
is the inverse of the string length ratio), as is the general practice today. For
example, suppose that the open string gives the note C_4 (Sa) = 512 cycles per
second. To obtain D_4 (Re), which is one major tone above it (a frequency ratio
of 9/8), we shall have to shorten the string by one ninth of its length. The eight
ninths remaining give the note D_4 (Re). To calculate the frequency, we have D_4
(Re) = 9/8 of C_4 (Sa) (that is to say, the inverse of the string-length proportion).
Thus, D_4 (Re) = 512 x 9/8 = 576 cycles per second.

This simple and accurate system has one defect, which comes from the
difficulty of knowing the relative sizes of intervals without making calculations.
For example, the major half tone corresponds to 16/15 and the minor half tone
to 25/24. We can easily see that the minor half tone is the smaller of the two

intervals. But is the difference between two whole tones and a fourth, the Greek limma (256/243), bigger or smaller, and in what proportion? We cannot, without calculation, know that it is in fact halfway between the two.

If we represent the notes by their frequencies, it will not make things any easier, because the frequencies, being inversely proportional to the string lengths, do not allow a direct comparison of intervals either. For easier reading and comparison of intervals, it is necessary to replace lengths and frequencies by numbers that are related to intervals on a linear scale—that is to say, by the logarithms of string-length or frequency ratios.

If we take the logarithm (base 10) of the frequency ratio and, for convenience, multiply it by one thousand, we shall have the interval expressed in terms of the unit known as the savart.[1] The Chinese use a similar but less convenient system based on decreasing powers of three.

The interval of the octave (Sa to upper Sa) is equal to two when expressed as a ratio of frequencies, since a rise in pitch of one octave corresponds to a doubling of the frequency of vibration of the sound (or to a halving of the string length). The logarithm of two being 0.30103, the interval of the octave is equal to 301.03 savarts or, with an accuracy sufficient for most purposes, 301 savarts.

This system makes the comparison of intervals very easy. For example:

the minor half tone (25/24) is approximately equal to 18 savarts,
the major half tone (16/15) to 28 savarts,
the Greek limma (256/243) to 23 savarts.

We can immediately see that the limma is situated between the minor and major half tones, at one comma (81/80 = 5 savarts) from each.

The American system, which is more and more widely used, divides the tempered half tone into 100 parts to give a unit known as the cent; the octave is thus divided into 1,200 cents. This system has certain defects. If we wish to use logarithms to ascertain the frequency ratio of an interval, it is tempting simply to divide the number of cents in the interval by four. Unfortunately this gives an inaccurate answer, since the octave is thereby divided into 300 parts instead of 301. The main defect of the cent, however, is that its definition is based on the tempered scale, which always brings errors and does not allow the true nature of intervals to be understood.

The Scale of Sounds

If we collect all the intervals that in ordinary practice are used in modes (rāgas), as well as in chords in relation to a note considered as the tonic, we shall obtain a certain number of points within the octave, each corresponding to a perfect relation to the tonic, though they may not have harmonious relations between themselves. If the same process is applied to each of the notes of the diatonic scale (*Sa* or *Ma grāma*), in relation to each note we shall obtain another set of points, some of which will coincide with those of the first set, and some of which will not. We shall thus obtain a number of distinct points within the octave, and we can then see whether they bring out a simple division of the octave and whether the points that form a harmonic interval with one note are also in a harmonic relation with other notes.

By trying all the possible combinations of the minor tone (10/9), the major tone (9/8), and the major half tone (16/15) and all the intervals resulting from their sums or differences, we find that the minor half tone (25/24) is the difference between the minor tone (10/9) and the major half tone (16/15), the limma (256/243) is approximately equal to the difference between the major tone (9/8) and the major half tone (16/15), the maximum tone (8/7) is approximately equal to the difference between the ditone (two major tones) and the minor tone, and so forth. We thereby obtain a division of the major tone into nine intervals, the minor tone into eight and the diatonic (major) half tone into five. These intervals are each of one comma (81/80 = 5 savarts) except for a discontinuity of eight savarts between the notes of different names (for example, C and C♯ [Sa and komal-Re], E and F [Ga and Ma], and so on). If we relate this scale to the keyboard of the piano or organ, we shall have several notes separated from each other by one comma (5 savarts) for each key, black or white, but between the highest note corresponding to a certain key and the lowest one corresponding to the next key there remains an interval of eight savarts.

If we divide that interval of eight savarts into two, we obtain, according to Western interpretation, the enharmonic sharp (or quarter tone) and the major enharmonic sharp (three-quarter tone) distant from the neighboring sounds in the scale by four savarts, or slightly less than a comma.

Notation

The system of notation we shall adopt is as follows:

The sign + indicates that the note is raised by a comma (81/80 = 5 savarts).

Thus D┤ (Re+)

The sign ++ indicates that the note is raised by two commas (10 savarts).

Thus D++ (Re++)

The superscript ♯ (sharp) indicates that the note is raised by a minor half tone (25/24 = 18 savarts). We have thus moved across the discontinuity of eight savarts, and in the example given, the note is no longer called D, but D♯ or E♭.

Thus D̊♯ = E̊♭ (Ga♯) (ati-komal)

The sign L- indicates that the lower note is raised by a limma (256/243 = 23 savarts), or the upper note lowered by a major half tone (16/15 = 28 savarts).

Thus $\overset{\text{L-}}{\text{C}}$♯ = $\overset{\text{L-}}{\text{D}}$♭ (ReL-) (komal)

The sign L+ indicates that the lower note is raised by a major half tone (16/15 = 28 savarts) or the upper note lowered by a limma (256/243 = 23 savarts).

Thus $\overset{\text{L+}}{\text{C}}$♯ = $\overset{\text{L-}}{\text{D}}$♭ (ReL+) (komal)

In the minor tone (which is equal to two limmas, that is, 46 savarts), L+ and L- are the same and are indicated simply by L.

Thus $\overset{\text{L}}{\text{D}}$♯ = $\overset{\text{L}}{\text{E}}$♭ (GaL) (komal)

The superscript ♭ indicates that the upper note is lowered by a minor half tone (25/24 = 18 savarts) or that the lower note is raised by a major half tone in the minor tone or by a large half tone (27/25 = 33 savarts) in the major tone.

Thus $\overset{\text{♭}}{\text{D}}$♯ = $\overset{\text{♭}}{\text{E}}$♭ (GaL) (komal)

The sign — indicates that the note is lowered by two commas (10 savarts).

Thus D— (Re—)

The sign – indicates that the note is lowered by one comma (81/80 = 5 savarts).

Thus D– (Re–)

To these signs are added, as previously explained, between ++ and ♯, the quarter tone, indicated by the sign ¼ and, between ♭ and —, the three-quarter tone, indicated by the sign ¾.

The major tone, the minor tone, and the diatonic half tone thus may be represented as in figures 1–3.

Figure 1. THE MAJOR TONE

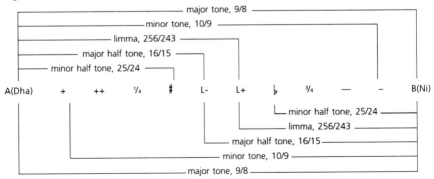

or

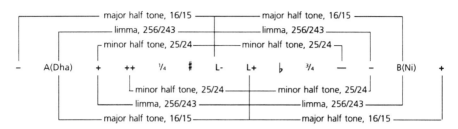

FIGURE 2.   THE MINOR TONE

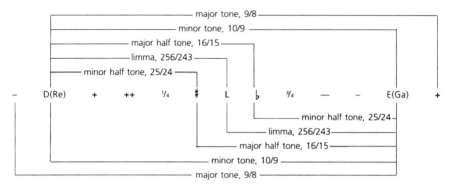

or

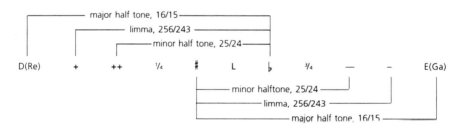

Figure 3.   THE DIATONIC HALF TONE

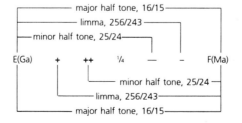

In practice, we shall indicate the exact tuning sign above the note, and the general indication sharp (♯) or flat (♭) beside the note as is customary. But in the Indian notation, as no doubt can arise, we shall generally indicate the exact tuning sign only.

We shall thus have $\overset{♯}{B♭}$, $\overset{L-}{B♭}$, $\overset{L+}{B♭}$, $\overset{♭}{B♭}$, etc.

(komal $\overset{}{Ni♯}$, NiL-, NiL+, Ni♭, etc.)

$\overset{♯}{A♯}$ would be identical to $\overset{}{B♭}$, $\overset{♯}{A}$ identical to $\overset{L+}{B♭}$,

$\overset{L-}{A♯}$ identical to $\overset{L-}{B♭}$, and so on.

In this way we obtain a division of the octave into fifty-three intervals, allowing us to play accurately—that is, without beats—all the usual harmonic intervals. And we can, with the help of this scale, notate accurately all the modes (*rāgas*) of all the musical systems. By *musical* systems we mean such systems as are used by musicians everywhere, and not such constructions of pure arithmetic as the tempered quarter tone.

We can note here that the fifty-three intervals of the scale of fifths (see chapter 4), if we want to use them musically—that is, sing them or play them by ear on a nonkeyed instrument—are automatically transformed into the simpler harmonic intervals, which are much easier to appreciate and much more natural. We might add that to sing without accompaniment the tempered scale is an undertaking beyond human capacities, because we cannot, without strong external help, escape from harmonic intervals, which alone are in accordance with the physical nature of sounds and consequently with the shapes and possibilities of the organs by which we can emit and perceive them.

"The tone or musical interval," the Arab theorist al-Fārābi once said, "can be agreeable, composed, or imagined,"[2] which may mean that there are intervals that are in conformity with harmonic laws (agreeable), intervals resulting from the relations between other intervals (composed), and intervals that may appear possible in theory but that cannot be used in practice. Such intervals can be conceived but cannot be executed by ear, and for this reason do not belong to the musical field proper, which is what interests us here.

Being limited to simple ratios, the acoustic intervals in use among the different human or animal races are, by the very nature of things, limited in number. But the modern "scientific" outlook, opposed to all hierarchy, considers the "agreeable" interval conforming to physical laws as being on an equal footing with any other interval, imagined or calculated. Such an outlook is quite astonishing to one who is not used to such egalitarian conceptions. Raouf Yekta Bey remarks, "The views and ideas of Western musicians about the scale appear to Easterners highly surprising and impossible to understand. For example, we hear of several scales under the names of Pythagoras, of Ptolemy, of Aristoxenes, of Zarlino, of the physicists. This may be all right. But is it the right of everyone to constitute a scale according to his own wishes and to ask people to sing according to the proportions of that scale? If nobody can do it, where do all these different scales come from? . . . The work of a theorist is to *measure* human song to find out its laws, and not to write, on *a priori* grounds alone, an artificial scale composed of any ratios he may care to adopt."[3]

This was also what Aristides Quintilianus thought: "The work of the musician consists not so much in comparing sounds as in assembling and bringing in tune all that Nature contains in her bosom."[4]

Harmonics

We are taught in primary school that we can subtract or add only things of like nature. In the same way, in the field of sounds we can establish logical relations only between sounds of like nature. Before we can study the relations between sounds, it is essential for us to know their nature. And for this, we must first examine the accessory sounds that form the natural superstructure of every individual sound, for their properties will necessarily be the basis for the practical construction of musical relations.

It is very difficult to produce a pure sound, because along with any sound we always hear a group of harmonics whose frequencies are exact multiples of the fundamental sound. The first harmonics form a triad, which is the logical basis of all music, and their intervals are the easiest and most natural to sing. Certain wind instruments, horns in particular, can play only the harmonics of their fundamental sound.

Generally, the further these harmonics are from the fundamental sound, the fainter they are. But according to the material used and the means employed to cause the vibration, certain harmonics may resound more strongly than others.

All possible frequency ratios are included in the unlimited series of harmonics. There is thus no harmonic or melodic combination that is not implied in the very structure of a single sound. This is, of course, a logical necessity, because there cannot be an effect whose potentiality is not contained in the cause, nor therefore an effect of sounds whose principle is not implied in every element of sound. Incidentally, this observation allows us to note the comparative unimportance of art forms whose development is necessary only because of our inability to perceive these inherent principles.

All possible ratios of sounds, being included in the series of harmonics, can be represented quite naturally by a relation of harmonics. We thus find that the major tone C-D (Sa-Re) = 9/8 is the interval from the 8th to the 9th harmonic; the minor tone D-E (Re-Ga) = 10/9 is the interval from the 9th to the 10th harmonic; the minor half tone, 25/24, is the interval from the 24th to the 25th harmonic, and so on. The tempered half tone can be seen as the interval from the 1,000,000,000th to the 1,059,463,094th harmonic.

The harmonics that are very near to the fundamental sound are the only ones that the human ear readily perceives and appreciates. Their relations appear more pleasing to us and normally form the elements of musical systems, because their correspondence with cosmic laws (the macrocosm) and with the physiological data peculiar to humankind (the microcosm) enables them to evoke ideas and images for us, which these ratios represent in simplified form. The further the harmonics are from the fundamental sound, the more they appear complicated and dissonant to us. This is because the numbers that form the first harmonics conform to the universe as our senses can perceive it. They form the legitimate human field in the magic world of sounds—the field that is open to us through the physical laws we depend on and the organs we possess, which are themselves in conformity with these laws. To those ideas, those images that we can evoke through sounds, we cannot give a tangible existence; without the knowledge of the transcendental laws of numbers, of which the perceptible laws of our illusory world give only an imperfect and approximate image, we cannot materialize them. But this knowledge is not normally accessible to us. The totality of these laws constitutes the tree of science, which it may be illegitimate and dangerous to approach.

The Scale of Harmonics

Although the harmonic series implicitly contains all the possible intervals used in music, the order in which those intervals appear does not properly constitute a musical scale. This is theoretically obvious, because the harmonic series as such has only one dimension; it is therefore unfit for even a simplified representation of the world of forms.

The harmonic series has often been proposed by physicists and acousticians as a basic scale, but its practical inadequacy quickly becomes clear. The main difficulty is that all its intervals differ from one another and become smaller as the scale rises. The harmonic series in its basic form is thus contrary to any form of modulation, and the fixed structure of tetrachords, the Aristotelian "body of harmony" indispensable for the establishment of musical scales, cannot be established.

Nevertheless, the series of the first sixteen harmonics can be considered to form a peculiar mode. When we deal with the meaning of musical modes we shall explain its remarkable significance. This mode can be generated by taking in turn the notes of the harmonic series and lowering each one by a whole number of octaves in order to bring it within a distance of one octave from the starting note.

If we take as a basis C (Sa), we first notice the appearance of the octave, C (upper Sa) 2/1, then the fifth, G (Pa) 3/2, then the third, E (Ga) 5/4, then the harmonic B♭ (komal Ni) 7/4—lower than the usual B♭ (komal Ni) and forming with upper C (Sa) the maximum tone 8/7. After this appears the major second, D (Re) 9/8, which forms with E (Ga) a minor second 10/9. Then come the harmonic F♯ (Ma¼) 11/8, A— (Dha—) 13/8, and finally, the seventh, B (Ni) 15/8. The remaining eight of the first sixteen harmonics add no new notes, as they are at exact octave intervals from earlier harmonics in the series. Considering only the first sixteen harmonics, we thus obtain a scale of eight tones formed of the following intervals:

	C	D	E	F♯	G	A—	B♭	B	C
	(Sa)	(Re)	(Ga)	(Ma¼)	(Pa)	(Dha—)	(NiL-)	(Ni)	(Sa)
Ratios:		9/8	5/4	11/8		3/2	13/8	7/4	15/8	2/1
Savarts:		51	46	41		38	35	32	30	28

The ratios are given in relation to C (Sa), and the intervals in savarts are those between one note and the next.

The harmonic series is not limited to the first cycle. It proceeds indefinitely, though theoretically, beyond the limits of perception. Figure 4, starting from C_0 (which equals thirty-two cycles per second), shows the first thirty-two harmonics in the order in which they appear.

Figure 4. THE HARMONICS OF C (SA)

No.	Western	Swara	Ratio	Freq.
1	C_0	Sa_0	1/1	(32)
2	C_1	Sa_1	2/1	(64)
3	G	Pa	3/2	(96)
4	C_2	Sa_2	4/2	(128)
5	E	Ga	5/4	(160)
6	G	Pa	6/4	(192)
7	B♭	Nil-	7/4	(224)
8	C_3	Sa_3	8/4	(256)
9	D	Re	9/8	(282)
10	E	Ga	10/8	(320)
11	F#¼	Ma¼	11/8	(352)
12	G	Pa	12/8	(384)
13	A—	Dha—	13/8	(416)
14	♭B♭	Nil-	14/8	(448)
15	B	Ni	15/8	(480)
16	C_4	Sa_4	16/8	(512)
17	♭D♭	ReL+	17/16	
18	D	Re	18/16	
19	♭E♭	GaL	19/16	
20	E	Ga	20/16	
21	F—	Ma—	21/16	
22	F#¼	Ma¼	22/16	
23	F#	Ma♭	23/16	
24	G	Pa	24/16	
25	A♭	Dha♯	25/16	
26	A—	Dha—	26/16	
27	A+	Dha+	27/16	
28	♭B♭	Nil-	28/16	
29	B♭¾	Ni¾	29/16	
30	B	Ni	30/16	
31	B¼	Ni¼	31/16	
32	C_5	Sa_5	32/16	

The numbers in parentheses correspond to the frequencies of the harmonics based on C_0 = 32 cycles per second.

Chapter Four

THE CYCLE OF FIFTHS:
THE MUSICAL
THEORY OF THE CHINESE

*What we hear is either
auspicious or inauspicious;
music must not be
inconsiderately executed.*

Sima Quan

Chinese Music

Chinese musical tradition certainly shares a common origin with the Indian tradition. The two systems are different applications of universal principles that are not only necessarily common to them but whose first enunciation seems also to have been the same. Traces of this common origin can be found in their respective essential theories, as well as in many technical expressions. Further, since the dawn of its history, China has had constant cultural exchanges with India; there are many "historical" proofs of this, even if one does not accept as historical the conquest of China by the hero Rāma, or the marriage of Nakula (the brother of Yudishthira) with the daughter of the king of China. But it seems that in the periods more accessible to modern means of investigation, contacts between the two countries became rare and the two cultures took very different directions. While India's music theorists were restricting themselves to the system of relations to a tonic, almost completely ignoring polyphony, the Chinese, on the contrary, were pursuing only the cyclic system, which necessarily leads to transposition. Thus the two countries became musically isolated and unintelligible to each other. This was certainly not the case fifteen or twenty centuries ago, when exchanges of orchestras between the two were quite common, as many documents, mostly Chinese, attest.

The Nature and Purpose of Music

Like the Indians and the Greeks, the Chinese recognize that music is a perceptible representation of the relations that connect the different elements of manifestation. This representation, when sufficiently accurate, can in turn act upon these relations and modify the course of events. "Music acts on the universe, heaven, and earth, and on all the beings contained therein."[1] "Being the expression of natural harmonies, music is a translation of the moral forces that are also a part of the universe; it arises from it but regulates it in turn. This aspect of the world's system has been profoundly analyzed and minutely exposed first by the classical books, then, later, by philosophers and historians. The *Yue ji* studies these questions from every point of view. It points out, on the one hand, similarities and essential relations between psychological, social, or political facts, and on the other, notes, instruments, melodies, songs, etc."[2] "The ancient kings . . . have established in the *lü* the proportions of what is small and what is big and classified the beginning and the end so as to represent the duties to be performed."[3] In spite of its far-reaching possibilities, the knowledge of these subtle relations does not generally have as its aim the transgression of cosmic limits or the escape from the endless cycle of life and death. The Chinese do not have that passionate desire for union with the Absolute that haunts the Indians. To them it seems essential to maintain order and harmony in our material world, and to achieve the perfect proportions in individual and social life that only the knowledge of the subtle correspondences between things can allow, harmonizing them with the help of appropriate sounds. "Music expresses the accord of heaven and earth . . . [and] produces harmony between men and spirits."[4]

"The physical laws of sound represent the social laws of hierarchy and union; they symbolize, prepare, and support good government. We might be tempted to see in these formulas a series of metaphors; the Chinese have seen in them, from the very beginning . . . the expression of real, tangible relations."[5] "He who sings becomes straight and displays his moral influence, and when he himself comes into motion, heaven and earth respond, the four seasons are in harmony, stars and planets are orderly, life is sustained in all beings."[6] This is why the mastery and ordinance of music are the first duties of politicians, because "if it is given to the dukes and ministers to hear the *lü* of each month in the court's assemblies, they will become able to move heaven and to accord themselves to the earth's influx."[7]

Yin and Yang

Since the Chinese musical system has as its only aim the establishment of contacts and mutual reactions between apparently unconnected aspects of manifestation, it is essential, if we are to understand its applications, to get an idea of the knowledge that the Chinese had of metaphysical reality and an idea of the book that sums up that knowledge, the *I ching*. Though it may seem to be a digression, it is necessary to give here a very short account of it.

Composed by the mythical emperor Fu Xi in the fourth millenium B.C.E., the *I ching* has been and still remains the inexhaustible source whose form conditions all Chinese metaphysical thinking.[8]

All manifestation issues from two supplementary and concordant principles, one positive, spiritual, active, male, and warm—the *yang*; the other negative, material, passive, female, and cold—the *yin*. These two terms correspond to the Sanskrit *linga* and *yoni*, which symbolize Śiva and Śakti, that is, *purusha* and *prākriti*, being and matter. These two principles are the basis of all existence. Any science must therefore begin with the definition of their respective position and proportion in the object of its study. It is with the study of this proportion that the scientist or artist should begin any enterprise, and this is particularly true of music, which is the most direct representation of the process of the world's creation.

> Jing Fang [about 45 B.C.E.] . . . had studied the *I ching*, the book of cosmogony and predictions, deeply with Jiao Yanshou. He was also learned in astrology and acoustics, since natural sciences are connected with the study of this canonical book. Following the steps of his teacher, he explained the theory of the progression of the *lü* [the cycle of fifths], not stopping after the twelfth tube as is customary, but proceeding up to the sixtieth. He based his system on the analogy of the eight *gua* or mystical trigrams of the *I ching*, which, united two by two, form sixty-four distinct combinations. Similarly the twelve original *lü*, multiplied by five, the number of elements, form in all sixty *lü*.[9]

The *I ching* represents the *yang* and the *yin* symbolically by a full line ——— and a broken line — —. These two lines can be combined in four different ways, forming the four *xiang* or digrams, as follows:

      ═══   extreme positivity (light, heat, etc.)

      ══ ━   small positivity (planets)

      ━ ══   small negativity (stars)

      ══ ══   extreme negativity (moon, cold, etc.)

These four digrams, applied to manifested forms, can be compared to the three fundamental qualities or *gunas* of Indian philosophy, which condition the whole of existence. Thus:

    ═══   *sattva*: ascending tendency, conformity to the pure essence of being

    ══━ or ━══   *rājas*: expanding tendency, development

    ══ ══   *tamas*: descending tendency, obscurity, degradation

From these four digrams issue the eight trigrams, which are:

☰ *qian* (heaven)	☳ *zhen* (thunder)
☷ *kun* (earth)	☴ *sun* (wind)
☱ *dui* (marsh)	☵ *kan* (water)
☲ *li* (fire)	☶ *gen* (mountain)

The principles represented by these eight trigrams find their application in the diverse aspects of manifestation. In the sixth chapter of *The Ten Strokes of the Wings*, Confucius gives the following correspondences for the eight trigrams:

Qian (heaven): activity, horse, head, father, all that is round, sun, prince, gold, cold, ice, red, swift horse, white horse, dry tree, what is straight, dress, speech

Kun (earth): passivity, mare, womb, mother, cloth, axe, economy, equality, the mother of the bull, cart, appearance, crowd, handle, black, what is square, bag, pipe, fly

Dui (marsh): he-goat, mouth, girl, child, diviner, tongue, rupture, hardness, concubine, duration

Li (fire): vibration, pheasant, eye, wife, sun, thunderbolt, woman, posterity, weapon, tortoise, stomach, reptile, fruit, stem, cow

Zhen (thunder): movement, the feet, the male principle, dragon, thunder, yellow, causal influence, highway, the elder son, haste, bamboo, harmonious song, mane, rebirth, repetition, crow

Sun (wind): entrance, hen, thigh, the female principle, wood, the elder daughter, thread, white, work, length, height, branch, the sense of smell, broad forehead, profile, tree, search

Kan (water): fall, pig, ear, husband, hidden secret, roof, bowstring, indisposition, blood circulation, pale red, ardor, light foot, cover, calamity, mood, thief, hardness of heart, den, music, thorny bush, weasel

Gen (mountain): stop, fox, hand, boy, path, stone, door, monk, finger, mouse, solidity, nose, tiger, wolf [10]

These trigrams, combined two by two, form sixty-four hexagrams, which allow the representation of all aspects of existence. It is through them that we can study and bring into practice the laws of correspondence between the different aspects of the world and, in the field of music, understand the modalities according to which the hierarchical succession of fifths will allow us to reach all the planes of the visible and invisible world, influence spirits, celestial emperors, elements, and seasons, and regulate the destinies of the empire. This is possible because "rites and music rise up to heaven and surround the earth, act upon the principles of *yin* and *yang*, and communicate with the *manes* [spirits of the ancestors] and heavenly spirits."[11] "Music . . . shakes heaven and earth, moves the spirits, brings into accord the two cosmogonic principles, penetrates men and *manes*."[12]

The correspondence of the trigrams to musical notes will vary depending on the method used to determine this correspondence, each method being valid in its own field. The comparison can, for example, be based on their symbolism, individually or in combination, or it can be based on an analysis of the trigrams' structure and the relative positions of broken and unbroken lines as compared with the structure of tetrachords and chords. The peculiarity of the trigrams is that, in whatever way they are manipulated, the endlessly various results will always be in conformity with some aspect of reality.

The Seven Degrees of the Pentatonic Scale

Chinese people have always been realists. They willingly conceive of abstract principles, but only to find immediate applications for them. The *I ching* itself, with its metaphysical trigrams, may have survived the persecution of scholars only because of its magical applications.

The ancient Chinese were certainly not ignorant of the transcendency of the heptatonic scale, which was assimilated by them to the "seven beginnings" (*qi shi*). However, since they conceived of music only as a means of harmonizing the elements of terrestrial existence and establishing a balance between spirit (heaven) and matter (earth), they did not pay much attention to the seven degrees, which form the scale of transcendental worlds; on the contrary, they cultivated to its utmost potentiality the science of the pentatonic scale, which symbolizes the opposing forces of heaven and earth, of *yang* and *yin*, held in equilibrium in the dualism of existence.

Many modern authors, carried away by the theory of evolution, want to make the heptatonic scale into a late development of a more "primitive" pentatonic form. As there is no concrete basis on which such a theory can be built, I do not propose to discuss it. We need only note that in the Chinese system (the only important pentatonic system of our times), although priority is evidently given to the first five notes in the cycle of fifths, which correspond to the five elements and which alone can be expressed by whole numbers according to the traditional definitions, this priority in no way implies that the two auxiliary degrees are not known or used. In Indian theory, music issues from seven sounds uttered by the seven *rishis* or sages, and connects in turn with the seven *dvīpa* or continents, which symbolize the seven successive aspects of the world's manifestation characterized by the seven colors of the spectrum. Unless we are ready to accept the idea that the "primitive" spectrum had only five colors, which is obviously absurd, it is difficult to see why things should be different for sounds. In reality, the laws that regulate the division of sounds, like those of light, are physical laws and not mere attributions, and it is only through ignorance that we may believe them to be arbitrary.

Furthermore, the *Shu jing* and the *Han shu* admit of the seven notes from the earliest times:

> At the date 522 B.C.E. the Zuo zhuan relates a conversation between the prince of Shi and Yan Zi, who enumerates the five degrees, the six *lü*, and the seven sounds, and commentators see in the seven sounds the five principal degrees and the two supplementary ones. The *Guo yu*, in a quotation from the musician Zhou Jiu, [a contemporary of King Jing (544–20 B.C.E.)], explains by the seven degrees, which it calls the seven *lü*, the date of the battle that King Wu won against the Yin. Whatever might be the value of such astrological considerations, they clearly indicate that four or five centuries before the Christian era, the existence of the seven-note scale was acknowledged as having existed since the beginning of the Zhou,[13]

which by no means precludes an earlier existence. Again, "the crown prince Sheng . . . declares that the seven-note scale has been known since the time of the emperor Shun (twenty-third or twenty-first century B.C.E.). The seven notes were then called the seven beginnings or *qi shi*. This expression is found in a passage of the *Shu jing*, quoted by the *Han shu*: "The *Shu jing* says, 'I wish to hear the harmony of the six *lü*, the five degrees, the eight sorts of instruments, the seven beginnings.'"[14]

These seven *qi shi* might well correspond to the seven *rishis* of Indian tradition, the deformation of the word followed by the attribution of a somewhat different meaning being not unusual for the passage of Vedic or Sanskrit words into Chinese.[15]

Symbolic Representation of the Pentatonic Scale

The earth, or visible world, is symbolized by the number four, which can be visually represented by the square. The earth is made of four perceptible elements, and all its characteristics are regulated by the number four (four seasons, four directions of space, four castes, etc.). But these four elements issue from one unique and celestial element, ether (*ākāśa*), of which they are only the modalities. Similarly, all matter exists only in relation to a single principle of manifestation. This projection of the single into the multiple is symbolically represented in Egypt, as well as in America and China, by the pyramid, whose square base seems to issue from the summit (the summit can also be represented by its projection at the center of the square).

Music, being the representation of the relationship between heaven and earth, must quite naturally have this configuration of a center or tonic (*gong*) surrounded by four notes assimilated to the four directions of space, the four perceptible elements, the four seasons, and so on.

The pentatonic scale thus presents a structure that allows it to be an adequate representation of the static influence of heaven on earth. But a static representation of a world in motion could not be an instrument of action upon that world. It is necessary, if we want to act upon the represented elements, to evolve from the motionless to the moving, from the angular to the circular, from the square to the circle. To express the movements of the universe, the sounds will have to submit to the cyclic laws that, in their own field, are represented by the *cycle of fifths*.

The Spiral of Fifths

As we have already seen, the fifth is the third sound of the series of harmonics, the first being the fundamental and the second its octave. According to the formula of the *Tao-te ching* ("One has produced two, two has produced three, three has produced all the numbers"),[16] we can understand why the third sound, the fifth, must necessarily produce all the other sounds by its cyclic repetitions. The first to be produced will be the four principal sounds, which form comparatively simple ratios with the tonic (ex. 1). They are:

$$\text{II} \quad \text{G (Pa)} = 3/2$$
$$\text{III} \quad \text{D (Re)} = 9/8$$
$$\text{IV} \quad \text{A+ (Dha+)} = 27/16$$
$$\text{V} \quad \text{E+ (Ga+)} = 81/64$$

Example 1

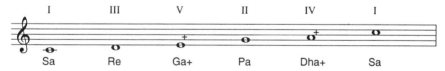

I	III	V	II	IV	I
Sa	Re	Ga+	Pa	Dha+	Sa

To these five primary sounds, whose disposition represents the elementary structure of the perceptible world, can be added the two auxiliary sounds:

$$\text{VI} \quad \text{B♭ (Ni+)} = 243/128$$
$$\text{VII} \quad \text{F♯ (MaL+)} = 729/512$$

Thus is formed the seven-note scale in example 2.

Example 2

I	III	V	VII	II	IV	VI	I
Sa	Re	Ga+	MaL+	Pa	Dha+	Ni+	Sa

But the two auxiliary sounds should not be used as fundamentals, because they belong to the scale of invisible worlds, and so we can neither perceive their accuracy nor build systems upon them without going out of tune:

At the date 541 B.C.E. Zuo relates a consultation given by He, physician of the land of Xin, to the marquis of Jin, then ruling: . . . "Beginning from the central sound, if we diminish [the length], after five diminutions, playing [on the instruments] is no longer allowed." Cai Yuangding sees in this text the law, imperative in ancient times, that allows the building of systems only on the five principal degrees. . . . The diminution of length indicates the passage to the fifth above, and in the series of fifths, the sixth degree obtained is a complementary degree and therefore inadequate for the foundation of a system.[17]

As we shall see later, the fifth successive fifth, whether in an ascending or a descending series, represents the limit of consonance in modal music also. Beyond this limit, no interval can appear harmonious, nor can it be accurately recognized. A rule originating from the same principle was also known in medieval Europe, where the tritone was prohibited as diabolical, that is, as connected with forces that are supernatural and therefore uncontrollable.

After these seven notes, the next five notes generated by the series of fifths are:

VIII D♭ (Re komal)

IX A♭ (Dha komal)

X E♭ (Ga komal)

XI B♭ (Ni komal)

XII F+ (Ma+)

We now have twelve sounds, which divide the octave chromatically into twelve half tones.

The twelfth fifth (note 13) brings us back to the fundamental, but with a slight difference. It is higher than the fundamental by one comma, the Pythagorean comma ($3^{12}/2^{19}$ = 531,441/524,288 or 5.88 savarts). It is, therefore, in our notation, C+ (Sa+).

If we proceed further, the twelve following fifths will place themselves one comma above the former ones, and the 24th fifth (note 25) will be one comma above C+ (Sa+), that is, C++ (Sa++). In this way, successive series of twelve fifths will be placed one above the other at one-comma intervals, up to the 52nd fifth (note 53).[18] However, after the 52nd fifth, the octave is filled up and the 53rd fifth (note 54) comes out of the octave and inserts itself between the octave C (Sa) and the twelfth fifth C+ (Sa+), thus forming, above C (Sa), a small interval of 0.84 savarts. Thus begins a new cycle, which in its turn, with a period of 53 fifths, will divide the octave into small intervals of 0.84 savarts. The next cycle will appear during the seventh series of 53, when the 359th fifth (note 360) comes out of the octave and forms, with C (Sa), an interval of 0.47 savarts. The next cycle is of 666 notes, with a basic interval of 0.035 savarts. Then comes a cycle of 25,524 notes with a basic interval of 0.0021174 savarts. This cycle is very near to that of the precession of the equinoxes, or the Pythagorean great year, which is of 25,920 solar years. The small difference between the twelfth fifth and octave, similar to that of the lunar and the solar year, leaves the door open for further cycles.[19]

In practice, for reasons that are symbolic as well as musical, after the 52nd fifth (53rd note) the Chinese follow the series only for the next seven degrees, which place themselves above those of the initial seven-note scale, and they stop the series at the 60th note. The reason given is that 12 (the number of each cycle) x 5 (the number of the elements) = 60.

This scale of fifths, perfect for transposition because of its extreme accuracy, also allows the study of astrological correspondences and of terrestrial influx, provided one possesses knowledge of the hierarchy of its intervals. "In the same melody, the prime, the third, the fifth, the sixth, are chosen independently because of their connection with diverse constellations and, consequently, with heavenly spirits, earthly spirits, and *manes*."[20]

Taking as the tonic any one of the notes of the first cycle, a scale of five notes can be obtained that form simple ratios (harmonic relations) with the tonic. The two auxiliary degrees already form somewhat troublesome ratios, and the others can be used only if the tonic is changed. The scale of fifths is therefore invariable and does not allow the study of harmonic proportions and chords.

Equalized or Tempered Divisions

Considering the first series of fifths, we can obtain the six perfect tones (five fifths and the tonic):

I	C (Sa)	II	G (Pa)	III	D (Re)
IV	A+ (Dha+)	V	E+ (Ga+)	VI	B+ (Ni+)

and the six imperfect tones (sharps and flats and the imperfect fourth):

VII	F♯ (Ma tīvra)	VIII	D♭ (Re komal)	IX	A♭ (Dha komal)
X	E♭ (Ga komal)	XI	B♭ (Ni komal)	XII	F+ (Ma+)

These can be considered as alternately masculine and feminine, as shown in Figure 5.

If we neglect the small difference between the thirteenth fifth and the octave, we obtain the equalized chromatic division into twelve half tones on which all *temperaments*, or equalized divisions of sound, space, and time, are based. The spiral is thus transformed into a circle, and the six perfect tones can

Figure 5.   THE SPIRAL OF FIFTHS

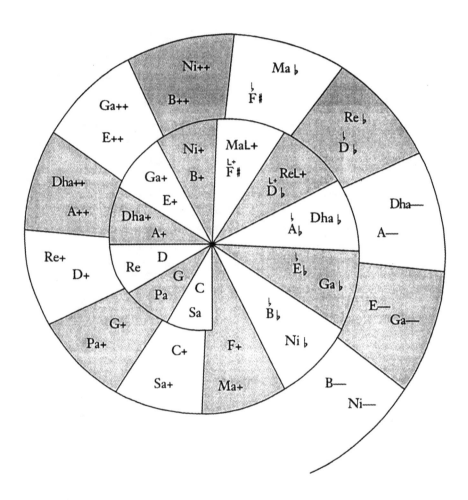

The shaded sections represent feminine notes.

be represented by the sides of an inscribed hexagon. If we divide the side of the hexagon (which is equal to the radius) first into two, then into ten parts, this will lead us to the division of the circle first into twelve then into sixty parts, divisions that are always employed for the representation of the world's movement within a closed circle. Westerners use this division for the measurement of circles and angles (60 x 6 = 360 degrees) and, consequently, for astrology and astronomy (the twelve signs of the zodiac, for example; see fig. 6). We use a similar division for time, dividing the day into twice twelve hours, the hour into sixty minutes, the minute into sixty seconds, and so on—divisions that are said to have been borrowed from the Chaldeo-Assyrians.

Westerners also divide the octave into twelve, but do not proceed with the logical implications of this division as the Chinese do. In reality, the physical laws that apply to sounds are not peculiar to them but are those which regulate all the normal rhythms of the universe. Those "rational" minds that smile at such notions might nevertheless be very embarrassed if Saturday did not come every seventh day, if the days no longer had twenty-four hours or the hours sixty minutes, and if the relation of the sun to the moon no longer formed a cycle of twelve months with a slight difference comparable to that between twelve fifths and seven octaves.

The Lü

The ancient Chinese did not make use of any scale other than that formed by the first five notes of the series of fifths, but they observed that if they wished to form a similar scale for transposition, starting from any note other than the fundamental, four additional notes were necessary. These notes form a continuation of the cycle of fifths, and this is what led the Chinese to take as the basis of their music the series of the first sixty fifths, which divide the whole structure of the octave into what Westerners call Pythagorean commas. "The scholar Chen Zhongru . . . demonstrates the impossibility of transposition if one is limited to the original twelve *lü*."[21]

As standards for the sixty notes in the octave, tubes of metal of extremely precise dimensions had been made since the remotest antiquity, giving sounds of fixed pitch, which are called *lü* and are the indispensable basis of Chinese music. Any of the *lü* can be taken as a tonic provided that there are other *lü* accurately tuned to form the pentatonic scale.

"The five degrees, born from the principles *yin* and *yang*, divide themselves between the twelve *lü*, which by their revolutions produce the sixty *lü*. It is by those diverse agents that the influx of the 'Bear' can be regulated and the relations between beings manifested. Heaven manifests itself in the seasons, earth manifests itself in sounds, that is to say, in the *lü*. If the *yin* and the *yang* agree, then when the seasons come, the influx of the *lü* responds."[22]

Figure 6. CYCLIC DIVISION INTO TWELVE

showing the correspondences with the zodiac, months, seasons, hours, minutes, octave, angles, etc.

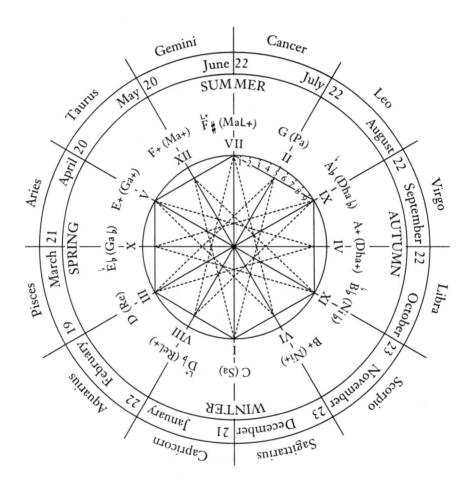

In this figure the order of succession of the fifths is given by the sides of the central star dodecagon. Each angle is connected by a dotted line to its upper fifth and its lower fifth. The notes that correspond to the angles of the hexagon are masculine; the notes that correspond to the middle of the sides are feminine.

The accurate measurement of the *lü* is obviously of fundamental importance, since not only the perfect relations of sounds depend on it but also the
standard pitch taken as a basis for the whole system. "If, to measure the five
degrees of the scale, the foot corresponding to the fiery element is used, fire
becomes important; . . . with the metal foot, weapons are important; with the
water foot the *lü* are in perfect tune, the empire is at peace."[23]

The Degrees of the Scale

Arising from the principles of *yin* and *yang*, the fifths thus engendered are
alternately of feminine and masculine character. Each note has a double character, one permanent as a *lü*, that is to say, as a particular frequency, the other
variable, according to its rank as degree in the scale (tonic, fifth, fourth, etc.).

A rise in the standard pitch, such as that which has occurred in Europe
during the last two centuries, must therefore, according to the Chinese, considerably change the influence, if not the expression, of music. It is always to such
variations that the fortune or the fall of dynasties can be attributed.

The notes in the series obtained by an ascending fifth (lower generation)
are of feminine character, and those obtained by a downward fourth (upper
generation) are masculine. According to the *Lü shi chun qiu*, the most ancient
text on the *lü*: "To the three parts of the generator, one part should be added to
form the upper generation [an increase in length in the ration of 4/3, giving a
drop in pitch of a fourth]; from three parts of the generator one part should be
taken off to form the lower generation [a decrease in length in the ratio 2/3,
giving a rise in pitch of a fifth]."[24] This is also in conformity with the Indian
theory on the active character of the fifth and passive character of the fourth.

Let us note here that the most striking difference between the system of
fifths and that of harmonic relations to a tonic resides in the perfect fourth,
which is an essential interval in the scale of proportions. The scale of fifths has
an augmented fourth as its sixth fifth, the interval of a fourth appearing only, in
a slightly augmented form F+ (Ma+), as the eleventh fifth, or, almost perfect, as
the fifty-second fifth. But if, instead of starting from C (Sa), we had begun one
fifth below, that is to say, from F (Ma), we would have obtained this essential
note without changing anything in our scale, except that, since we begin with
a masculine interval instead of a feminine interval, the character of the whole
system is modified. This is not merely an arbitrary attribution, but corresponds
to a fundamental difference in musical expression that the Indians express by the
difference between the Sa and the Ma *grāmas* (the tonic on the fundamental or
on the fourth) and the Greeks by the difference between the modes in which the
mesa (middle note) is the tonic and those in which the fundamental is the tonic.
Herein lies the inner difference of significance between the two Dorian modes,
between the Lydian and the Hypolydian, and so on.

"The five notes, according to Sima Qian, correspond to the five *lü* [known as] *huang zhong, tai cu, gu xian, lin zhong,* and *nan lü*—the only ones whose measurements can be expressed by whole numbers, starting from the base 81."[25]

"The numbers given by the Chinese to correspond with the relative length of the tubes in the pentatonic or five-tone scale are 81, 54, 72, 48 and 64 . . . these numbers hold great cosmological significance in Chinese culture, as do the numbers 3 and 2, which symbolize heaven and earth respectively."[26]

The first four fifths, which form "simple" ratios with the tonic, are, from the most ancient origins, the five degrees of the Chinese scale:

I   *gong*   C (Sa)   1/1   = 81/81
II   *zhi*   G (Pa)   3/2   = 81/54
III *shang*   D (Re)   9/8   = 81/72
IV   *yu*   A+ (Dha+) 27/16 = 81/48
V   *jiao*E+ (Ga+) 81/64   = 81/64

We see that the Chinese numbers are the denominators of these ratios and therefore correspond to acoustic reality as well as to the necessities of symbolism.

To those degrees are added, by two new fifths, the two auxiliary degrees, which no longer correspond to whole numbers on the basis of 81. They are:

VI   *bian gong* (modified *gong*) or *he* (auxiliary)
= 81/64 x 3/2 = 243/128 = B+ (Ni+)
VII *bian zhi* (modified *zhi*) or *miu* (different)
= 243/128 x 4/3 = 729/512 = FL+♯ (MaL+)

The Scale of the Lü

Since the *lü huang zhong* is the fundamental (*gong*), we shall consider it as corresponding to C (Sa), because of its traditional use as the general tonic, although according to Father Amiot its frequency is of 708.76 cycles per second, which makes it an F♯ (Ma♯) on the scale of the physicists, or an F natural in modern Western pitch. "*Gong*, source of light, the center to which everything is attracted, corresponds to the sound we call F."[27]

To be able to represent the intervals of the first twelve notes of the cycle of fifths by whole numbers, the Chinese take the length of an open string (or pipe) sounding the *huang zhong* as equal to $177,147 = 3^{11}$ units. The first fifth (*lü* II) will be 2/3 of that number, that is, $3^{10} \times 2 = 118,098$.

The next fifth, brought back within the octave (*lü* III), will be 4/3 of this new number, that is, $3^9 \times 2^3 = 157,464$.

The following fifth (IV) will be 2/3 of the preceding number, that is, $3^8 \times 2^4 = 104,976$.

The following fifth (V) will be 4/3 of the preceding number, and so on.

The fifths whose numbers in the series are even (II, IV, etc.) are feminine, and the fifths whose numbers are odd (I, III, V, etc.) are masculine.

"Six of the *lü* bear especially the name of *lü* (rules), or *zhong* (middle, medium): they are those whose rank in the series is odd; they depend on the male principle, *yang*. The six others, whose rank is even, depend on the female principle, *yin*, and are called *lü*[28] (helpers), or, in a more ancient form, *tong* (companions), or *jian* (intermediaries)."[29] The representative numbers of the fifths go on in this way until the twelfth *lü*, F+ (Ma+) = 2^{17} = 131,072. Thereafter, the numbers are no longer integers, as this number is not divisible by three, but can be represented by whole numbers with a degree of approximation similar to that of ordinary logarithms (savarts).

If we follow the endless development of the series of fifths, it will lead us, octave after octave, into vibratory regions that no longer belong to the realm of perceptible sounds and where the various successions and groupings of vibrations will take ever new and unexpected forms. These particular properties of the vibratory scale constitute the key that reveals the difference in the nature of the vibrations at different stages, perceived as sound, light, touch, taste, or smell, and finally the structure of matter and of the atom itself, as envisaged by the Indian grammarians.

The graphic representations of the cycle of fifths at its different stages will give us successively all the important symbolic and geometrical constructions. Within the range of sound we already obtain, as primary graphic representations, the square, the pentagon, the dodecagon, the circle, the spiral, the labyrinth, the zig-zag, and so forth.

We cannot enter here into a lengthy study of the properties of the powers of the ratio 3/2 and its graphic representations. Figure 7 presents the succession of the sixty *lü* according to the system of Jing Fang (c. 45 B.C.E.).

Symbolism and Correspondences of the Lü

Western readers should be warned against making any hasty judgments about the practical value of the correspondences attributed to musical notes by the Chinese or the Indians. These attributions are by no means arbitrary and are perfectly in accordance with the inevitable significance of musical intervals, although they often refer to certain kinds of correspondences that we are not accustomed to consider. Their application can be found in every music—and in particular in Western music—in a way that may appear almost systematic, as in Wagner, or instinctive, as in Beethoven, Liszt, or Chopin. And it is necessary that it should be so, because the descriptive value or the emotional significance of all music depends on these correspondences.

The Chinese system of correspondences is logical and coherent. We can unfortunately only glance at it here.

Figure 7.   SCALE OF FIFTHS (THE SIXTY _LÜ_)

Lü	Order in the succession of fifths	Degree	Name of the _lü_	Ratio	Chinese number	Savarts	Interval
1	I	C (Sa) gong	_huang zhong_	1	$177,174 = 3^{11}$	0	tonic
2	(LIV)[a]	...	_(se yu)_	$3^{53}/2^{84}$	$176,777\ldots = 2^{83}/3^{42}$	(0.84)	...
3	XIII	C+ (Sa+)	_zhi shi_	$3^{12}/2^{19}$	$174,762\ldots = 2^{18}/3^{1}$	5.88	Pythagorean comma
4	XXV	C++ (Sa++)	_bing sheng_	$3^{24}/2^{38}$	$172,410\ldots = 2^{37}/3^{12}$	11.74	two commas
5	XXXVII	D♭ (Re ♯)	_fen dong_	$3^{36}/2^{57}$	$170,089\ldots = 2^{56}/3^{254}$	17.61	minor half tone
6	XLIX	D♭ (Re L−)	_shi mo_	$3^{48}/2^{76}$	$169,800\ldots = 2^{75}/3^{37}$	23.48	limma
7	VIII	D♭ (Re L+) sharp gong	_da lü_	$3^{7}/2^{11}$	$165,888 = 3^{4} \times 2^{10}$ or 2/3 of VII	28.52	major half tone
8	XX	D♭ (Re♭)	_fen fou_	$3^{19}/2^{30}$	$163,654\ldots = 2^{29}/3^{8}$	34.38	large half tone
9	XXXII	D−− (Re—)	...[b]	$3^{31}/2^{49}$	$161,451\ldots = 2^{48}/3^{20}$	40.35	small tone
10	XLIV	D− (Re−)	...	$3^{63}/2^{68}$	$159,278\ldots = 2^{67}/3^{32}$	46.12	minor tone

[a] Figures in parentheses refer to fifths above the fifty-second (note LIII), which form with the adjoining notes intervals smaller than a comma.
[b] It has not been possible to trace any source listing the names of all the sixty _lü_; our own list is therefore unfortunately incomplete.

				$3^2/2^3$			
11	III	D (Re) *shang*	*tai cu*	$3^2/2^3$	$157,464 = 3^9 \times 2^3$ or 4/3 of II	51.14	major tone
12	(LVI)	...	...	$3^{55}/2^{87}$	$157,136\ldots = 2^{86}/3^{44}$	(51.99)	...
13	XV	D+ (Re+)	*shi xi*	$3^{14}/2^{22}$	$155,344\ldots = 2^{21}/3^3$	57.07	large tone
14	XXVII	D++ (Re++)	...	$3^{26}/2^{41}$	$153,253\ldots = 2^{40}/3^{15}$	62.89	...
15	XXXIX	E♭ (Ga‡)	...	$3^{38}/2^{60}$	$151,190\ldots = 2^{59}/3^{27}$	68.76	small minor third
16	LI	E♭ (Ga L)	...	$3^{50}/2^{79}$	$149,155\ldots = 2^{78}/3^{39}$	74.63	trihemitone
17	X	E♭ (Ga♭) sharp *shang*	*jia zhong*	$3^9/2^{14}$	$147,456 = 3^2 \times 2^{13}$ or 2/3 of IX	79.68	major third (major tone + apotome)
18	XXII	E— (Ga—)	...	$3^{21}/2^{33}$	$145,471\ldots = 2^{31}/3^{10}$	85.53	...
19	XXXIV	E– (Ga–)	...	$3^{33}/2^{52}$	$143,512\ldots = 2^{51}/3^{22}$	91.401	small major third
20	XLVI	E (Ga)	...	$3^{45}/2^{71}$	$141,581\ldots = 2^{70}/3^{34}$	97.37	major third
21	V	E+ (Ga+) *jiao*	*gu xian*	$3^4/2^6$	$139,968 = 3^7 \times 2^6$ or 4/3 of IV	102.31	ditone
22	(LVIII)	...	...	$3^{57}/2^{90}$	$139,676\ldots = 2^{89}/3^{46}$	(103.14)	...
23	XVII	E++ (Ga++)	*bian yu*	$3^{16}/2^{25}$	$138,084\ldots = 2^{24}/3^5$	108.17	large major third

Lü	Order in the succession of fifths	Degree	Name of the lü	Ratio	Chinese number	Savarts	Interval
24	XXXIX	F—' (Ma—)	...	$3^{28}/2^{44}$	$136,225\ldots = 2^{43}/3^{17}$	114.04	...
25	XLI	F– (Ma–)	...	$3^{40}/2^{63}$	$134,391\ldots = 2^{62}/3^{29}$	119.91	small fourth
26	LIII	F (Ma)	yi xing	$3^{52}/2^{82}$	$132,583\ldots = 2^{81}/3^{41}$	125.78	fourth
27	XII	F+ (Ma+) sharp jiao	zhong-lü	$3^{11}/2^{17}$	$131,072 = 2^{16}$ or 2/3 of XI	130.81	large fourth (fourth + Pythagorean comma)
28	XXIV	F++ (Ma++)	nan zhong	$3^{23}/2^{36}$	$129,307\ldots = 2^{35}/3^{12}$	136.68	...
29	XXXVI	$\overset{\sharp}{F}\sharp$ (Ma ♯)	...	$3^{34}/2^{55}$	$127,566\ldots = 2^{54}/3^{24}$	142.55	small augmented fourth
30	XLVIII	$\overset{L}{F}\sharp$ (Ma L–)	...	$3^{47}/2^{74}$	$125,849\ldots = 2^{73}/3^{36}$	148.42	harmonic tritone
31	VII	$\overset{L+}{F}\sharp$ (Ma L+) pyen zhi or myeu	rui bin	$3^6/2^9$	$124,416 = 3^5 \times 2^9$ or 4/3 of VI	153.46	cyclic tritone (3 major tones)
32	(LX)	...	...	$3^{59}/2^{93}$	$124,156\ldots = 2^{92}/3^{48}$	154.29	...
33	XIX	$\overset{\flat}{F}\sharp$ (Ma ♭)	sheng bian	$3^{18}/2^{28}$	$122,741\ldots = 2^{27}/3^7$	159.42	large augmented tone
34	XXXI	G— (Pa—)	...	$3^{30}/2^{47}$	$121,088\ldots = 2^{46}/3^{19}$	165.19	...
35	XLIII	G– (Pa–)	...	$3^{42}/2^{66}$	$119,459\ldots = 2^{65}/3^{31}$	171.06	small fifth

			lin zhong	3/2	$118{,}098 = 3^{10} \times 2^{1}$ or 2/3 of I	176.09	fifth
36	II	G (Pa) *zhi*	*lin zhong*	3/2	$118{,}098 = 3^{10} \times 2^{1}$ or 2/3 of I	176.09	fifth
37	(LV)	...	...	$3^{54}/2^{85}$	$117{,}852.. = 2^{84}/3^{43}$	(176.93)	...
38	XIV	G+ (Pa+)	*qu mie*	$3^{13}/2^{20}$	$116{,}508... = 2^{19}/3^{2}$	181.96	large fifth
39	XXVI	G++ (Pa++)	...	$3^{25}/2^{39}$	$114{,}940... = 2^{38}/3^{14}$	187.83	...
40	XXXVIII	A♭ (Dha♯)	...	$3^{37}/2^{58}$	$113{,}393... = 2^{57}/3^{26}$	193.7	small diminished sixth
41	L	A♭ (DhaL)	...	$3^{49}/2$	$111{,}867... = 2^{76}/3^{38}$	199.57	...
42	IX	A♭ (Dha♭) sharp *zhi*	*yi ze*	$3^{8}/2^{12}$	$110{,}592 = 3^{3} \times 2^{12}$ or 4/3 of VIII	204.61	diminished sixth (fifth + apotome)
43	XXI	A— (Dha—)	*jiao zhing*	$3^{20}/2^{31}$	$109{,}103... = 2^{30}/3^{9}$	210.47	...
44	XXXIII	A- (Dha-)	...	$3^{32}/2^{50}$	$107{,}634... = 2^{49}/3^{21}$	216.34	small sixth
45	XLV	A (Dha)	...	$3^{44}/2^{69}$	$106{,}185... = 2^{68}/3^{33}$	222.21	harmonic sixth
46	IV	A+ (Dha+) *yu*	*nam lii*	$3^{3}/2^{4}$	$104{,}976 = 3^{8} \times 2^{4}$ or 2/3 of III	227.24	cyclic sixth (fifth + major tone = 27/16)
47	(LVII)	...	...	$3^{56}/2^{88}$	$404{,}757... = 2^{87}/3^{55}$	(228.08)	...
48	XVI	A++ (Dha++)	*jie gong*	$3^{15}/2^{23}$	$103{,}563 ... 2^{22}/3^{4}$	233.11	large sixth

Lü	Order in the succession of fifths	Degree	Name of the lü	Ratio	Chinese number	Savarts	Interval
49	XXVIII	B♭ (Ni♯)	...	$3^{27}/2^{42}$	$102,169\ldots = 2^{41}/3^{16}$	238.98	small minor seventh
50	XL	B♭ (NiL-)	...	$3^{39}/2^{61}$	$100,794\ldots = 2^{60}/3^{28}$	244.85	seventh harmonic
51	LII	B♭ (NiL+)	yi ban	$3^{51}/2^{80}$	$99,437\ldots = 2^{79}/3^{40}$	250.72	minor seventh
52	XI	B♭ (Ni♭) sharp yu	wu yi	$3^{10}/2^{15}$	$98,304 = 3^1 \times 2^{15}$ or 4/3 of X	255.76	minor seventh
53	XXIII	B— (Ni—)	bi yan	$3^{22}/2^{34}$	$96,980\ldots = 2^{33}/3^{11}$	261.62	...
54	XXXV	B- (Ni-)	...	$3^{34}/2^{53}$	$95,675\ldots = 2^{52}/3^{23}$	267.49	small seventh
55	XLVII	B (Ni)	...	$3^{46}/2^{72}$	$94,387\ldots = 2^{71}/3^{35}$	273.36	major seventh
56	VI	B+ (Ni+) bvo or pyen gong	ying zhong	$3^5/2^7$	$93,312 = 3^6 \times 2^7$ or 2/3 of V	278.40	cyclic major seventh
57	(LIX)	...	...	$3^{58}/2^{91}$	$93,117\ldots = 2^{92}/3^{46}$	(273.24)	...
58	XVIII	B++ (Ni++)	chi nei	$3^{17}/2^{26}$	$92,056\ldots = 2^{25}/3^6$	284.26	large major seventh
59	XXX	C— (Sa—)	...	$3^{29}/2^{45}$	$90,817\ldots = 2^{44}/3^{18}$	290.13	...
60	XLIV	C- (Sa-)	...	$3^{41}/2^{64}$	$89,594\ldots = 2^{63}/3^{30}$	296.00	small octave

The first twelve notes of the series of fifths, or *lü*, divide the octave into twelve half tones corresponding to the different moons or months (see Figure 8):

The *da lü* (VIII), D♭ (ReL+), corresponds to the twelfth moon,

The *tai cu* (III), D (Re), corresponds to the first moon,

The *jia zhong* (X), E♭ (Ga♭), corresponds to the second moon, and so on.

"The *huang zhong* [I, fundamental = C, Sa], is the *lü* of the eleventh moon, that of the winter solstice. Of yellow color,[30] it corresponds to the element earth because in that season the *yang* influx, male and hot, is hidden in the earth."[31]

"The *huang zhong* [I] is used as the fundamental in the sacrifices to heaven because it is the *lü* of the eleventh moon and because, in that season, the vivifying influence of heaven begins to make itself felt. The *tai cu* [III, D, Re], is adequate for the sun because it is the male form of the *jia zhong*, which corresponds to the spring equinox; it is indeed at the time of the equinox that the sun is worshiped. The *huang zhong* [I, C, Sa], is assigned to the emperor, prince among men and image of heaven, the *nan lü* [IV, A, Dha], to the empress."[32]

The Chinese scale, being invariable, constitutes in effect a single mode. Every change in expression or significance will therefore depend upon modulation, that is, a change of tonic. This is also true to a certain extent in Western music. According to Jing Fang:

> Each separate *lü* being the perfection of a day, the others are to be transposed according to their order, because the *lü* corresponding to the days are, in succession, the fundamental note. . . .
>
> Because there are twelve *lü* and twelve scales similar to the standard scale [of seven notes], there are eighty-four systems, of which sixty are for the principal modes and twenty-four for the complementary modes.[33]

"Among the twelve *lü*, seven sounds [degrees] are taken successively, which make a scale. . . . For each scale there are seven systems: in total eighty-four systems on which are based the melodies, sung or played."[34]

"For sacrifices at the altar of heaven, the *huang zhong* [I] should be taken as a fundamental [Sa]; for the altar of the earth the *lin zhong* [II]; for the temple of ancestors the *tai cu* [III]; for the ceremonies in the five suburbs, for the assemblies of congratulations, and for the court banquets, the *lü* of the month."[35]

According to the *Da king hui dian* (eighteenth century):

> The *huang zhong* [I] is fundamental for sacrifices to heaven and to the *shang li*. The *lin zhong* [II] is fundamental for the sacrifices to the earth. The *tai cu* is fundamental for sacrificing to the emperors or empresses of the ruling dynasty, and also to the sun and to the *tai suai* [the spirit of the

Figure 8.   SOME CORRESPONDENCES OF THE FIRST TWELVE LÜ

Note	Name of *lü*	Seven beginnings	Fundamental for sacrifices	Annual cycle	Gender	Moon
C (Sa)	*huang zhong* (I)	Heaven	to the *yellow* emperor, to heaven	winter solstice	masculine	11th (December)
C♯ (ReL♭+)	*da lü* (VIII)				feminine	12th (January)
D (Re)	*tai cu* (male form of *jia zhong*) (III)	Man	to the *white* emperor, to ancestors		masculine	1st (February)
E♭ (Ga♭)	*jia zhong* or *yuan zhong* (X)		to spring	spring equinox	feminine	2nd (March)
E+ (Ga+)	*gu xian* (V)	spring	to the *green* emperor, to the first agriculturalists		masculine	3rd (April)
F+ (Ma+)	*zhong lü* (XII)				feminine	4th (May)
F♯ (MaL+)	*rui bin* (VII)	summer		summer solstice	masculine	5th (June)
G (Pa)	*lin zhong* or *ban zhong* (II)	Earth	to the *red* emperor, to earth		feminine	6th (July)
A♭ (Dha♭)	*yi tze* (IX)				masculine	7th (August)
A+ (Dha+)	*nan lü* (IV)	autumn	to the *black* emperor, to the empress, to the moon	autumn equinox	feminine	8th (September)
B♭ (Ni♭)	*wu yi* (XI)				masculine	9th (October)
B+ (Ni+)	*ying zhong* (VI)	winter			feminine	10th (November)

year identified with the planet Jupiter]. The *nan lü* [IV] is fundamental for sacrifices to the moon. The *gu xian* [V] is fundamental for sacrifices to the First Agriculturists. In spring the *jia zhong* [X] is fundamental, and in autumn the *nan lü* [IV] is fundamental, for the sacrifices to the *tai she*, the *tai zi* [spirit protectors of the state territories], to the rulers of former dynasties and to Confucius. . . . When the emperor appears in the great hall of the throne for the three great yearly festivals, the fundamental is the *huang zhong* [I]; when the empress comes into the central palace on the occasion of the three great yearly festivals, the fundamental is the *nan lü* [IV]. For ordinary assemblies at the court, the *lü* of the month should be taken as fundamental. . . . Generally, there are melodies of nine repetitions (for sacrifices offered to the *shang ti*), of eight repetitions (for sacrifices performed at the altar of agriculture, the altar of the sun, the altar of the first agriculturists), of six repetitions (for sacrifices performed in the temple of ancestors, at the altar of the moon, etc.).[36]

"From the winter solstice to the summer solstice are the months born from the *yang* principle; in these months only half *lü* [high pitch] are used and no double *lü* [low pitch]. From the summer solstice to the winter solstice are the months of the *yin* principle; then are used double *lü* and no half *lü*, because the *yang* corresponds to one and the *yin* to two."[37]

"To the emperor and the prince corresponds the *huang zhong* [I, C, Sa], that is, the element earth. If the *huang zhong* is fundamental, the second [D, Re] suits the ministers. The fundamental expresses the majesty of the emperor."[35]

"The five regions of space are under the dominion of the five celestial emperors."[36]

Yellow emperor	*huang zhong*	I	C (Sa)	Center
Red emperor	*han zhong*	II	G (Pa	South
White emperor	*tai cu*	III	D (Re)	West
Black emperor	*nan lü*	IV	A+ (Dha+)	North
Green emperor	*gu xian*	V	E+ (Ga+)	East

The tonic A (Dha) is called by the Chinese *Hu xi* (western lamentation), a name that is in accordance with the melancholy character of the scale of A (Dha) (minor mode).

After the winter solstice, the fundamental is the lower C (Sa).

Before the winter solstice, the fundamental is the upper C (Sa).

The odd *lü* are masculine, the even *lü* are feminine.

The meanings of the names of the first twelve *lü* are given on page 53, and some of their correspondences are summarized in figure 9.

Figure 9. CORRESPONDENCES OF THE DEGREES OF THE SCALE

Degree	Note	Color	Direction	Element	Season	Numbers	Function	Animal and quality
gong fundamental	C (Sa)	yellow	center	earth		5	emperor and prince	naked species
shang major second	D (Re)	white	west	metal	autumn	9 and 4	ministers	hairy species (the white tiger of the west) metallic sound, firm and rigid unbearable for spirits
jiao major third	E+ (Ga+)	blue	east	wood	spring	8 and 3	people	scaly or aquatic species (the blue dragon of the eastern sea)
miu or *bian zhi* (modified *zhi*) augmented fourth (tritone)	L+ F♯ (MaL+)							
zhi fifth	G (Pa)	red	south	fire	summer	7 and 2	public services	feathered species (the red bird of the south)
yu sixth	A+ (Dha+)	black	north	water	winter	6 and 1	products	shelled species (the black turtle of the north)

Meanings of the Names of the First Twelve Lü According to Du Yu (∂. 812 C.E.)

Huang zhong, C (Sa)

Ḥuang zhong = yellow bell. Yellow is the color of the element earth. In this season (winter solstice), the *yang* influx, male and hot, is hidden in the earth.

Da lü, C ♯ (ReL+)

Da = large

Tai zhi, D (Re)

Tai = great; *zhi* = to arrive, multiply. During the first moon, all beings come to life under the *yang* influx.

Jia zhong, E♭ (Ga♭)

Jia = to help (in relation to heaven), therefore the synonymous *yuan,* circle, the symbol of heaven.

Gu xian, E+ (Ga+)

Gu = dried up, old; *xian* = washed, fresh. During the third moon all beings are renewed.

Zhong lü, F+ (Ma+)

Zhong = middle (or *xiao* = inferior)

Rui bin, F ♯ (MaL+)

Rui = luxuriant vegetation; *bin* = to treat as a guest. The *yang* influx begins to give place to the *yin* influx.

Lin zhong or *han zhong,* G (Pa).

Lin = forests. During the sixth moon the forests are flourishing.
Han = to envelop. This is an allusion to celestial action.

Yi ze, A♭ (Dha♭)

Yi – to wound, *ze* = rule, chastisement. In the seventh moon, all beings begin to feel the hardships of winter.

Nan lü, A+ (Dha+)

Nan = to support. Plants are less luxuriant and appear oppressed (eighth moon).

Wu yi, B♭ (Ni♭)

Wu = privation; *yi* = impulse, production. With the approach of winter, nature closes in and concentrates itself.

Ying zhong, B+ (Ni+)

Ying zhong = the bell that answers.

Correspondences of the Degrees of the Scale

"Notes begin to have a musical value when a certain number of them, chosen for reasons of perceived affinities, form a scale or melodic progression. The chromatic series . . . is therefore not, properly speaking, musical, as each sound is put into a neutral state in relation to the others. . . . The *lü*, the material of music, acquire meaning when some of them are chosen as degrees of a scale." Only then does their significance become clear and can their symbolism be definitely perceived and understood." The *Yue ling* bring out the connection between months and elements, the *lü* on one side and the five degrees on the other, and, finally, the numbers from five to nine."[40]

We shall give below some of the correspondences of the notes considered as degrees of the scale. These correspondences will be maintained in transposition whatever may be the *lü* corresponding to the fundamental degree (*gong*).

"The element earth, which has no corresponding season, is nevertheless connected with a degree, a *lü*, a number."[41]

"The five degrees of the scale are assimilated to the prince, the ministers, the people, the works, the material resources; but the prince being superior to the minister, it is necessary that the corresponding note be lower than that of the minister."[42]

> The *gong* degree (tonic) represents the prince.
>
> The *shang* degree (second) represents the ministers.
>
> The *jiao* degree (third) represents the people.
>
> The *zhi* degree (fifth) represents public works.
>
> The *yu* degree (sixth) represents the products.

"If the five degrees are not disturbed, there will be no discordant sounds."[43]
The five notes correspond to the five natural agents:

> *Gong* (tonic) = center of the earth
>
> *Shang* (second) = metal and autumn
>
> *Jiao* (major third) = wood and spring
>
> *Yu* (sixth) = water and winter
>
> *Zhi* (fifth) = fire and summer[44]

"The *shang* degree is firm and rigid; . . . it has the sound of metal."[45]
According to the *Zhou li*:

> One and six are the numbers of water (shelled species).
>
> Two and seven are the numbers of fire (feathered species).
>
> Three is the number of wood and also that of the dragon
> of the eastern sea (scaly species).

Four is the number of metal and of the west (hairy species; the white tiger of the western hills).

Five is the number of the earth (naked species and spirits of the Earth).

Six is the number of celestial spirits.[46]

The colors of the five degrees are:

> Fundamental, C (Sa)—yellow
> Major second, D (Re)—white
> Ditone, E+ (Ga+)—blue
> Fifth, G (Pa)—red
> Sixth, A+ (Dha+)—black.

The dominant color in spring E+ (Ga+) is blue, the dominant color in summer G (Pa) is red, the dominant color in autumn D (Re) is white, and the dominant color in winter A+ (Dha+) is black.

Western Commentaries

With the prejudice of Westerners, who so often deny *a priori* all the scientific conceptions of other races until they are "rediscovered" by themselves and ceremoniously re-named in Latin or German, the Chinese division of the octave, however rational it may be, is ridiculed by most Western writers. Even Maurice Courant allows himself to write: "Needless to say, the sixty degrees in the octave are scarcely perceptible and are difficult to realize, a slight difference of temperature bringing a significant variation in the sound compared with the interval of two successive degrees. Such a scale can never be accurate."[47]

I do not know on what grounds Courant makes such a sweeping statement, which experiments could easily have proved unfounded. If he were to tune two strings corresponding to the same note of his piano with one comma of difference, he would then see whether this interval is perceptible, and I cannot believe that his piano plays such dreadful tricks with every change of temperature. We should not forget that the problem is not to play intervals of one comma in succession but to play intervals with an accuracy of one comma. A difference of one comma in a fifth or an octave is not only perceptible but extremely disagreeable even to an untrained ear. The same difference in a third or in a major second (it is then the difference between the major and the minor tone) completely changes the color of the note and its expression. One can even say, as a rule, that such differences are the very basis of vocal and melodic expression, whether one is conscious of it or not, as can easily be verified with accurate instruments for the measurement of frequencies.

Western scholars have two obsessions, into whose framework they wish to force all the facts. One is the theory of evolution applied to the short period of recorded history. The other, sometimes called the "prejudice for classicism," pretends that everything whatsoever comes from the Greeks. To give an instance of the former, they remain undisturbed by the fact that their musical theory is extremely nebulous and often in contradiction to elementary acoustic laws, and find it quite natural to believe that it is by mere chance that the Chinese have for thousands of years been using a perfectly scientific theory. As an example of the prejudice for classicism let me quote Maurice Courant again: "It seems that an entirely new musical system has been substituted for the rudimentary carillons in which China had hitherto taken delight. As this system is exactly that of the Pythagoreans, and it makes its appearance in the Far East after the expedition of Alexander, one would be inclined to believe that it was a result of the influence of Greek civilization in China."[48]

Courant is here simply repeating the words of other orientalists who claim that Chinese music developed as a result of a Greek military expedition to the Indus. It is impossible to treat seriously such poetic flights of fancy, which show only a very weak knowledge of geography. There is no doubt that the Chinese system is similar to that of Pythagoras. But if an influence is to be considered, it was certainly in the opposite direction.

The immediate sources of Greek music were undoubtedly in the Near East, and the Phrygian and Lydian modes were so called not because Alexander taught them respectively to the Phrygians and the Lydians but because the Greeks borrowed them from those peoples. Besides, the travels of Alexander to the banks of the Indus can in no way affect Chinese culture, because to come from Macedonia to Bactria is a very simple journey compared with the enormous distance and the formidable obstacles that separate the Indus from Beijing.

A few scholars, however, take a diametrically opposite view. According to David and Lussy, "The musical system of the Greeks had certainly not originated in their country. . . . One is bound to suppose that Pythagoras brought from the East the musical system that was adopted by his countrymen of Hellas. . . . It was foreigners coming from India, Persia, and Asia Minor; the Phrygians Hyagnis, his son Marsyas, and Olympus; the Thracians Linos, Thamyris, and Orpheus, who imparted music to Greece. We therefore believe, until better information is obtained, that the Hellenic tonal system had its origin in India or perhaps in China; the Greek instruments were all of Asian origin, and we admit, with Fétis, that in music nothing belongs to the Greeks that cannot be found in the Orient in conditions of superiority that leaves them far behind. . . . Let us examine their instruments. . . . compare them with the abundant variety of instruments that the Orientals once possessed, and we shall be bound to recognize that the Greeks, so remarkable in other artistic fields, have been, of all the ancient peoples, the least proficient in those resources that are the essentials of a musical culture."[49]

These simple observations, which every available fact corroborates, should create at least some doubt in an unprejudiced mind with regard to the Greek origin of Eastern musical systems. But as we have already seen, this does not apparently disturb later scholars when they want to impose their prejudices. This ability to juggle facts and ignore all those views or proofs that contradict their opinion has made almost all the theories of Western scholars concerning the relations of Eastern and Western civilizations of ancient times absolutely untrustworthy. Indeed, in certain fields, accepted theories that are believed by most Westerners to be irrefutable truths amount to nothing less than a deliberate falsification of history.

~ *Chapter Five* ~

RELATIONS TO A TONIC: THE MODAL MUSIC OF INDIA

> *In this universe there is no form of knowledge that is
> not perceived through sound; knowledge is pierced through
> by sound; all this universe is but the result of sound.*
>
> *Vākya Padīya, 1.124*

> *Utterance (vāk) brought forth all the universe. He [God]
> pronounced "Bhū" and the earth was born. . . . From
> the sound of Vedas that supreme divinity made all things.*
>
> *Manusmriti, 1.21*

Indian Musical Theory

From the remotest antiquity, besides a general theory of sounds, a theory of musical modes has existed in India, which seems to have been the source from which all systems of modal music originated. Unlike other systems, the Indian theory is not limited to experimental data, nor does it arbitrarily consider certain modes or certain chords as "natural"; rather, it takes as its starting point the general laws common to all aspects of the world's creation.

Starting from metaphysical principles, the Indians have recreated the theory of sounds. They have analyzed and classified all possible ratios and relations between sounds. The result is obviously an astronomical number of theoretically possible chords, modes, and combinations, of which only a few are used in practice. The others, however, remain accessible for the day when new conditions or the inspiration of musicians may require new modes or new musical forms.

The Indian classification deals once and for all with the subject of musical relations. It is the necessary basis of any serious study. All other classifications are child's play beside it. Unfortunately its approach is difficult; no systematic study of it has been made in any modern language, and we cannot begin this enormous undertaking here. But without going beyond the limits of the classi-

~ 58 ~

fications used today in Indian music, we can find therein easily understandable elements, which are sufficient for the comparative study of all the existing modal systems.

The Laws of Music and their Applications

The theory of sounds can be approached in two ways: either as the systematic application of the universal laws of creation common to sound and other aspects of manifestation, or as the empirical use of physical peculiarities in the development of sounds. The first approach is called by the Indians *mārga* (directional) and, being based on absolute laws, is universal and unchangeable, while the other, which is called *deśī* (regional), varies endlessly according to place and time.

The power of a music constructed according to *mārga* rules is extraordinary, its influence over animate and inanimate things unlimited. In the words of the grammarian Bhartrihari, "This science of sounds is the chemistry of the universe." There is no sort of transformation in the structure or appearance of things that cannot be achieved through the influence of organized sounds.

Ritual music must necessarily follow the rules imposed by *mārga* theory. This is why most of the *mārga* definitions are kept in the ritual that regulates the singing of *Sāmaveda*. On the other hand, the object of *deśī* music is usually only pleasure or the expression of human feelings and passions, so *deśī* systems vary greatly from country to country and from time to time. Their influence may be good or bad. All modern musical systems are of this empirical and unstable kind, and their relative value can be measured only by comparing them with the permanent definitions of the *mārga* theory, which alone is based on absolute laws.

"The music that is called *gandhārva* (*mārga*) is that which has been from time immemorial practiced by the *gandhārvas* (celestial singers) and which leads surely to *moksha* (liberation), while the *gana* (*deśī*) music is that which has been invented by composers (*vaggeyakaras*), in conformity with recognized rules, and which pleases people. *Gandhārva* music always follows the rules of theory."[1]

"Music is of two kinds, *mārga* and *deśī*. The kind that was sought by Brahmā and other gods, and practiced by Bhārata and other sages in the presence of Śambhu (Śiva), is called *mārga*; it brings everlasting prosperity, while the songs, play, and dances that please the hearts of people in different countries are called *deśī* (regional)."[2]

Modal System and Harmonic System

Before starting the study of Indian music, and in order to be able to understand its meaning, we should fully realize the difference between modal and harmonic music. We should also give up the prejudice that sees in the harmonic form a development or "progression" from the modal form, with the accompanying notion that "progression" implies "progress." There is only a difference in the form of expression, which does not imply any superiority either in conception or in scope. In the words of Rāja S. M. Tagore, "There is nothing to make us regret that the principles of acoustics, as they exhibit themselves in our music, differ from the European system."[3] We must remember that, just as Indian musicians may see in harmony only a meaningless noise, Europeans are perhaps similarly incapable of appreciating the significance of an isolated modal degree. They cannot realize how an isolated note can convey the full meaning of a chord, because of its position in regard to the memorized tonic and sometimes to another axial note. Still, by the work of memory, a single note really does form a chord or relation of sounds. According to Vedantists, "a single sound is not capable of manifesting a meaning (*sphota*), otherwise to utter another sound would be useless . . . but, each sound leaving an impression (*samskāra*) in the mind, it is by the cumulative operation of the previous sounds (*dhvani*) that the last sound reveals the idea."[4]

Westerners, although they are bound to acknowledge this process in spoken language, are not trained to perceive it in musical language, and they recognize the meaning only if the few sounds that represent the idea are heard simultaneously. An exception can be made for the arpeggio, which can theoretically be understood in both systems. There is no essential difference between successive and simultaneous sounds, provided the ratios that bind them are the same. The image appears suddenly to our mind as soon as the different elements that constitute it have been perceived. It is the relation of sounds that represents the idea, and as long as this relation remains incomplete, the idea cannot appear, "the partial manifestation of a concept being impossible because a concept has no parts."[5]

The harmonic system, in which the group of related sounds is given at once, is in a way more direct, but it is also less clear, because an accurate discrimination of the different elements that constitute a chord is not usually possible. Modal development, on the other hand, allows the exact perception and immediate classification of every one of the sound elements. The modal system therefore permits a much more accurate, powerful, and detailed outlining of what the music expresses.

This is why the modal system is always to be given preference when music is envisaged not merely as a stimulant for sensations but also as a means of education capable of creating profound and durable impressions in the mind. This is easily explainable: an external perception can produce a permanent impression in our mind (*sthāyī bhāva*) only if we concentrate on it for a sufficiently long time. Only modal music can create such permanent impressions, because all its variations only tend toward the expression of one accurately determined feeling or image. This cannot fail, after a sufficient time, to imprint that feeling or that image in the mind of all those who hear the mode, whether they are attentive or not.

In Western music, all the notes have an approximately equivalent value because each note can be the root, fifth, or third of a chord. The significance of the notes as modal degrees is consequently virtually nil, and in any case extremely weak. In modal music, however, where modulation is virtually unknown, the idea of a third will always be represented by the third degree, the idea of a fifth by the fifth degree, and so on.

The result of this difference is that in modal music the modal degree will have the significance that is attached to the corresponding interval in harmonic music, degree and interval being the elements that in each case represent a permanent numerical relation. And we shall see that the Indians attribute to the modal degree almost exactly the same emotional and suggestive characteristics that Westerners attribute to the corresponding harmonic interval. The ancient Indians were aware of the equivalence of the two systems, and treatises insist that the same thing can be expressed by the succession of notes in a well-established mode or by the harmony of simultaneous sounds, the cosmic and emotional correspondences being the same in both cases.

The Problem of the Division of Sound

While the divisions of light (blue, red, yellow, etc.) or the divisions of taste (sweet, bitter, salty, etc.) seem to us obvious, the divisions of sound are the subject of constant controversy. Yet sounds, like the other phenomena by which we perceive the elements, are related by fixed laws, and their relations evoke in our mind precise images. Why then do we experience more difficulty in fixing the divisions of sound than we do the divisions of light? Westerners generally deny that there is a division of sounds in perfect accord with the rules of musical expression, as well as with the laws of acoustics, and they hide their ignorance behind the impressive word *psychology*. But this leads nowhere and flagrantly contradicts experience. A minor chord will never have for anybody the mood of a major one. If musical mood changes, it is only because the ratios between sounds change, and it is only the extraordinary ignorance of Western musicians as to the intervals that they are actually using which allows them to believe that they can give to a certain note a more or less expressive value by some mysterious transfusion of their "personality" without changing its pitch. The situation is further complicated by the use of instruments tuned to a tempered scale in which all the intervals are wrong in relation to the logical scale of sounds. This fact leaves room for doubts in interpretation, which performers and listeners may to a certain extent exploit according to their own tendencies—doubts that are impossible if the intervals are accurate. On tempered instruments such as the piano, to be able to give to any note a definite feeling or mood, it is necessary for the structure of the chords to compel us to interpret that note in a particular way, and this necessitates a mass of chords whose only role is to color the otherwise insipid notes of the tempered scale. Modern music is overcrowded by such chords, among which those chords that have a truly harmonic expression, meaning, or message seem lost.

The Theory of Elements

Indian metaphysics explains why it is difficult for us to perceive the natural divisions of sound and indicates the method by which we can realize them.

The world is composed of five elements,[6] which we perceive separately by five distinct senses. The sense corresponding to each of these elements can also perceive the lower elements but not the higher ones. Thus earth, whose corresponding sense is smell, can be perceived by all senses; water, which corresponds to the sense of taste, is perceived by all the senses except smell; fire (identified with light) corresponds to sight and cannot be tasted or smelled; air, which corresponds to touch, is no longer visible; and finally, ether can be perceived only through sound. Being unable to verify our hearing perceptions with the help of any other sense, it is impossible for us to justify the divisions of sound as we perceive them, because we can have no direct element of comparison.

Sound being a quality of ether, we can visualize it only through its reaction upon other elements, such as air, for example, of which the sensible quality is touch. We therefore easily represent sound as a vibration of air that, touching our ear, forces it to vibrate—a fact that is actually only a secondary phenomenon.[7]

The grammarians (Pāṇini, Patañjali) consider that air is the covering that prevents sounds, the vibration of ether, from being perceptible. Motionless air is opaque to sounds, and only when the air is made to vibrate does it allow the sound to pass, or temporarily become the vehicle of sounds.

Modern physicists observe that the speed of the sound wave, already lower in air than in most liquids and solids, becomes slower and slower as the temperature of the air drops, that is to say, when the speed of the molecules decreases. This may well bring us to the conclusion that at absolute zero, the interstellar absolute cold, the speed of the sound wave in still air would be nil.

> The ear cannot perceive air [which is perceived by the sense of touch], therefore the *Mīmāṃsakas* (the exponents of *mīmāṃsā*, the philosophical system of Jaimini) consider that air waves [literally, alternations of pressure and decompression], and consequently sounds, are not perceived by the ear as an air vibration. . . . Sound alone [devoid of all intellectual bearing] cannot be perceived. It is only the materialized idea (*sphota*) in the shape of sound (*dhvani*) that is perceived. . . . Words have a meaning and a sound,

the sound being only the external characteristic through which the meaning is grasped.

Still air is opaque to the perception of ideas (*sphota*).[8] When that opacity is removed [that is, when the air, being made to vibrate, becomes the vehicle of ideas], then it is said that sound (*dhvani*), which is the vehicle of the idea (*sphota*), should be considered only as a quality of the idea, that is, as an accessory phenomenon.[9]

Sound and Vibration

Hearing, as the sense corresponding to ether, is at the limit of our perceptions. Thus the natural and real divisions of sound are only experimentally demonstrable for us with the greatest of difficulty, unlike those of visible light, for example. This is why "rational" minds, who admit only that which is physically evident, have a tendency to suppose that the divisions of sound are arbitrary, while they would never say this about the colors of the spectrum. But such an attitude, which modern people believe to be rational, leads them to a conception that is materially inaccurate, since all peoples of all times will always fall back into the same divisions of the scale of sounds because those divisions are in accordance with reality. Differences exist only on paper and are due in the main to the ignorance of most musicians about the exact nature of the intervals they actually use. The much greater knowledge that the Indians had of the continuity of perceptible and nonperceptible planes has allowed them, by analogy, to define the divisions of sound with the most rational and scientific precision, while modern science proposes only arbitrary and illogical divisions because it does not go beyond the accessory phenomenon of gross vibration. This phenomenon, being itself only an effect, can neither prove nor show anything.

The modern approach renders every observation confusing and will never allow the establishment of a logical theory of sounds in accordance with musical reality. This will be easily understood by musicians who have reached the dead end that is formed by the representation of sounds by their frequencies, a representation that, although theoretically simple and accurate, places an insurmountable barrier of complication and inaccuracy in the way of any analysis of musical relations and "mystifies the subject by enveloping it in a cloud of mathematicism."[10]

The ratio of two sounds is of a different nature and only incidentally refers to their frequencies. The same ratio expresses the relative rank of the sounds in the scale of harmonics; 25/24, for example, is the interval between the twenty-fourth and the twenty-fifth harmonics. Inverted, it also represents the length ratio of pipes or strings used to produce the notes. These ratios are therefore the expression of general laws of sound that are applicable to the frequency of vibrations, but not exclusively so.

The Nine Svaras

The Indians consider the scale as made of seven principal notes, or *svaras*, connected with the seven main planets, and two secondary notes, corresponding to the nodes of the moon. This brings the total number of moving notes of the scale to nine, which are related to the nine groups of consonants of the Sanskrit alphabet.[11] These sounds place themselves, according to modes, into the twelve regions of the octave, just as the nine groups of consonants associate themselves with the twelve vowels, or the planets with the twelve signs of the zodiac.

The seven principal notes, or *svaras*, are called: Shadja (born of six), Rishabha (bull), Gāndhāra (pleasing to celestial beings), Madhyamā (middle sound), Pañchama (fifth note), Dhaivata (deceitful), and Nishāda (seated). In practice they are called more briefly: Sa, Re, Ga, Ma, Pa, Dha, Ni.[12] The two accessory *svaras* are named antara-Ga (intermediate Ga), and kākalī-Ni (pleasing Ni).

In the nomenclature of the *Yajurveda* the notes are called *udātta* (raised), *anudātta* (not raised), and *svarita* (accented). *Svarita* notes correspond to what Aristotle later called the "body of harmony"; they are the fixed notes that determine the upper and lower limits of the groups of four notes known as tetrachords. Of the two remaining notes within each tetrachord, the higher note is called *udātta* (raised), and the lower one *anudātta* (not raised).

According to the *Nārada-śiksā*, one of the most ancient texts on music, "Nishāda and Gāndhāra are born of *udātta*; Rishabha and Dhaivata are born of *anudātta*; and Shadja, Madhyamā, and Pañchama are born of *svarita*."

The scale is thus divided into two tetrachords as follows:

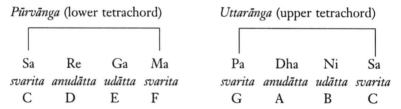

Pūrvānga (lower tetrachord)				*Uttarānga* (upper tetrachord)			
Sa	Re	Ga	Ma	Pa	Dha	Ni	Sa
svarita	*anudātta*	*udātta*	*svarita*	*svarita*	*anudātta*	*udātta*	*svarita*
C	D	E	F	G	A	B	C

In the classification of the *Sāmaveda* the notes are simply numbered, starting from Madhyamā, which is called Prathamā (first).

The seven notes are thus:

Prathamā	(first)	Ma	F
Dvitīya	(second)	Ga	E
Tritīya	(third)	Re	D
Chaturtha	(fourth)	Sa	C
Pañchama	(fifth)	Dha	A
Atisvara	(extreme note)	Ni	B
Krishta	(pulled, dragged)	Pa	G

According to the *Nārada-śikshā*, "The *svara* (note) that is Prathamā (first) in the singing of *Sāma(veda)* is the Madhyamā of the flute, Dvitīya is Gāndhāra, Tritīya is Rishabha, Chaturtha is Shadja, Pañchama is Dhaivata, Atisvara is Nishāda, Krishta is Pañchama."

We can see, therefore, that the scale of *Sāmaveda* is a descending scale with five principal notes and two secondary ones, while the later scale of profane music, given here as that of the flute, is a full seven-note ascending scale. We shall again meet the peculiar inversion of the Atisvara and Pañchama of the Vedic scale when we study the Pythagorean theory.

The Tonic and the Grāmas

The lowest note of the scale, which should be considered only as the auxiliary tonic, is the only tonic used in modern times. But in ancient books, the general tonic is always given as the fourth note, Madhyamā (middle sound), which corresponds to the *mesa* of the Greeks.

The tonic is the only note that cannot be modified or suppressed. There-fore "the destruction of Madhyamā should never be performed; Madhyamā is the best of all *svaras* and everlasting in the opinion of the sages who sing *Sāmaveda*."[13]

Madhyamā is an appropriate name for the general tonic because, accord-ing to the definitions of Vedānta, this name is given to "the fundamental per-ceptible sound from which all the differentiations of sound arise."[14]

In reality, the note taken as the starting point in the sequence of *svaras* varies according to our approach. If we deal only with terrestrial (*ādhibhautika*) music, the scale should begin from Sa (C), the first note. This is called *Shadja grāma* (scale of C). In the words of Rāmāmātya, "All the *deśī rāgas* are those of *Shadja grāma*."[15] But if we deal with celestial (*ādhidaivika*) music, the scale be-gins from Ga. This is called *Gāndhāra grāma* (scale of E). From the metaphysi-cal (*adhyātmika*) point of view, the scale begins from Ma. This is the *Madhyamā grāma* (scale of F). To understand this differentiation, we may remember that in a similar way the sequences of seasons, according to A. K. Coomaraswamy, "correspond to spring, summer, autumn, winter in *pratyaksha*, *adhyatma* sequence, or autumn, winter, spring, and summer in *paroksha*, *ādhidaivata* [angelic] se-quence: similarly, to infancy, youth, maturity, and age in our corporeal parlance, that is, to maturity, age, youth, and infancy, spiritually."[16]

The difference between the *Sa* and *Ma grāmas* is similar to the difference in Greek music between the two forms of the Dorian mode. In the first Dorian (*Sa grāma*) the fundamental is at the same time tonic and final, but in the second Dorian (*Ma grāma*), the modal fifth has for its fundamental the *mesa* (Ma), which thus becomes pseudo-tonic and fundamental, but without completely ousting the Sa, which remains final and becomes pseudo-dominant.

The Diatonic Series and the Comma Diesis

The shifting of the tonic from Ma (F) to Sa (C) is not an arbitrary operation, but corresponds to a peculiarity in the structure of the harmonic scale of sounds, similar to the Pythagorean comma in the cycle of fifths.

The diatonic scale is composed of three different kinds of interval—major tone, minor tone, and major half tone—which can be considered as forming an indefinite cyclic series of seven joint tetrachords of varying composition, as shown in figure 10.

Apart from tetrachord II, which contains three full tones (tritone), all the other tetrachords form a perfect fourth (major tone + minor tone +major half tone = 4/3), except for tetrachord V, which is too big by one comma (2 major tones + major half tone = 27/20 = 4/3 x 81/80). If we raise the A (Dha) by one comma to give A+ (Dha+), in order to make tetrachord V into a perfect fourth from A+ (Dha+) to D (Re), then tetrachord IV, from E (Ga) to A+ (Dha+), becomes too big. It is this particularity that is used by the *Natya-śāstra* to define the *śruti* as equal to one comma *diesis* (81/80—the difference between the major and the minor tone) from A (Dha) to A+ (Dha+) (ancient Pa– to Pa).[17] No greater accuracy in definition could be found because the perfect fourth (or its inversion, the perfect fifth) is an interval that cannot stand inaccuracy. If we tune two instruments according to the detailed instructions of Bhārata, we obtain an interval of one comma extremely accurately and without any difficult measuring. Later on, we shall see this method in detail. This shows, incidentally, that modern authors who pretend that the microtonal intervals (*śrutis*) are not clearly defined in Sanskrit treatises, and who interpret them according to the fancies of their own imagination, either have not read or have not understood the *Natya-śāstra*, or are not aware of the most elementary particularities of the diatonic scale. Thus we read remarks such as those of N. A. Willard to the effect that "several Sanskrit treatises are in existence, but they are so obscure that little benefit is to be expected from them to the *science*."[18] Willard, however, did not know Sanskrit.

The Tonic and the Cosmic Cycles

Quite independently of the differentiation of the *grāmas*—that is, of whether the first or the fourth note is taken as the tonic of each scale—the first note of the diatonic series itself varies through history. Thus all the notes of the diatonic scale are successively considered as the first note, that is, as Sa (C).

The scale given by the *Natya-śāstra* is, according to modern terminology, the scale of D (Re) in the diatonic series; it therefore necessarily belongs to a later period than the Greek scale, because the note that appears to be the logical tonic goes lower and lower as the cycle develops.

Figure 10. THE SEVEN TETRACHORDS OF THE DIATONIC SCALE

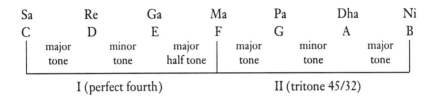

I (perfect fourth)   II (tritone 45/32)

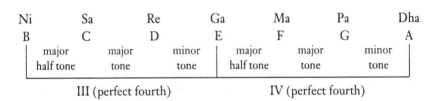

III (perfect fourth)   IV (perfect fourth)

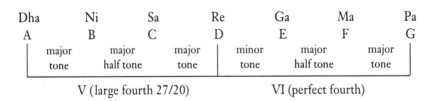

V (large fourth 27/20)   VI (perfect fourth)

VII (perfect fourth)

Example 3.

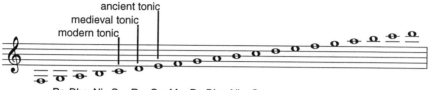

... Pa Dha Ni Sa Re Ga Ma Pa Dha Ni Sa ...

When we speak here of the tonic becoming progressively lower, we are not speaking of its absolute frequency, or of the phenomenon of changing standard pitch (although this too is far from being unimportant), but of the note chosen as general tonic in the unlimited diatonic scale. This note has been successively called, in modern terminology, E, D, and C (Ga, Re, and Sa; see ex. 3). The scale considered today as having no altered notes (*śuddha*) is the scale of C (Sa), which is the tonic of this particular time. In this modern scale, the Greeks would have called E (Ga) the fundamental. The ancient Egyptians would have given this name to F (Ma), while future generations will give it to B (Ni).

But this does not in any way affect the modes, as every note of the scale can be taken as a modal tonic; it only indicates the predominance of certain modes at certain times, in particular the major mode (which corresponds to *rāga Bilāval*) today, the mode of Re (*rāga Kāfi*; see ex. 4) in the Middle Ages, and the Dorian mode or mode of Ga (*rāga Bhairavī*; see ex. 5), in Greco-Roman times.

Example 4. *Kāfi*, or mode of Re (D)

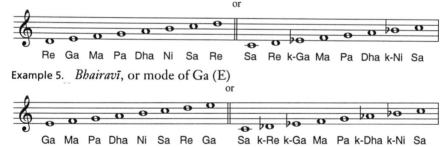

Example 5. *Bhairavī*, or mode of Ga (E)

If we consider the diatonic scale, given by the white keys of the piano or organ, the note that medieval authors would have called the tonic is the note that we today call D (Re), because they considered as unaltered (*śuddha*) the scale that has a minor third and a minor seventh (*Kāfi that*), while today we recognize only the major mode (*Bilāval that*) as the unaltered scale.

The Two Diatonic Scales

As we have seen, it is the adjustment of A (Dha) that differentiates the two forms of the diatonic scale. In the first form, the second tetrachord has intervals as follows:

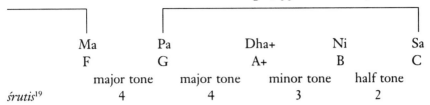

This is called *Sa grāma*, the scale of the tonic. It is, in modern notation, the mode of D (Re) because the fifth D A+ (Re Dha+) is pure, which is indispensable if Re is tonic.

The other scale presents the following succession:

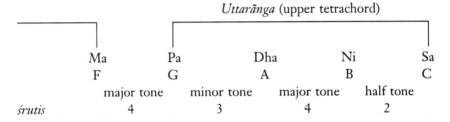

This is the (theoretical) modern Western major scale. It is called the scale of the fourth (*Ma grāma*) because its real tonic is G (Pa), which is the fourth of the scale of D (Re), the fundamental scale of Bhārata. The D (Re) could not be fundamental in this scale because its fifth would not be pure; the interval D to A (Re to Dha) equals 40/27.

"There are two *grāmas*, that of Sa [Re (D)] and that of Ma [Pa (G)], containing 22 *śrutis*. In the *Sa grāma* they appear in the order 3, 2, 4, 4, 3, 2, 4."[20] That is:

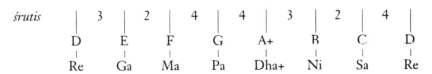

"In the *Ma grāma*, the Pañchama [Dha+ (A+)] must be lowered by one *śruti*. The difference of Pañchama is the very measure of *śrutis* [which can be described as a difference of] softness or accentuation, of expression or of length."[21]

Thus the *śrutis* of *Ma grāma*, starting from Sa (ancient Sa = Re [D]) are:

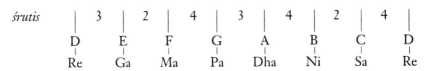

The Ga Grāma

In ancient times there was another, nondiatonic scale, based on a different principle, in which all the intervals except one were equal to three *śrutis*. But this scale, the *Ga grāma* (scale of the third), whose tonic was the modern note F (Ma), being the representation of celestial spheres, is in our corrupted times hidden from the eyes of ordinary mortals. There are some grounds to believe that it corresponds to a division of the scale of sounds according to numerical properties that in geometry are peculiar to the pentagon. The third, as we shall see later, is particularly connected with the number five. This division would also have been known to Pythagoreans, as is shown by the term *apotome* used for its characteristic interval, a term that for the Pythagoreans had a very particular significance in relation to the golden section and the pentagon. Euclid uses the same term to represent the irrational segment separating a regular and a proportional division of a straight line.[22]

The Scale of Nine Sounds and the Mūrchanas

The diatonic scale (*Sa* or *Ma grāma*) takes the form of a series of notes continuing indefinitely; as in example 6.

Example 6.

Sa Re-k Re Ga Ma Ma-t Pa Dha Ni Sa Re-k Re Ga Ma Ma-t Pa Dha Ni Sa

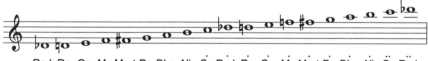

Re-k Re Ga Ma Ma-t Pa Dha Ni Sa Re-k Re Ga Ma Ma-t Pa Dha Ni Sa Re-k

If we take successively as the practical tonic the seven principal notes[23] of this scale, we shall obtain seven different plagal scales, or mûrchanas, which by eliminating some of their notes will be used for the establishment of expressive modes, or *rāgas*, of nine, eight, seven, six, or five notes. Most of the musical modes come within this classification.

The *mūrchanas* that contain only the seven principal notes are called *śuddha*, or pure *mūrchanas*. Those that make use of *antara-Ga* (Ma tīvra [F♯]), and thus have eight notes, are called *śuddha-antara mūrchanas*. The *mūrchanas* of eight notes that use only *kākalī-Ni* (Re komal [D♭]) are called *śuddha-kākalī mūrchanas*. If *antara-Ga* and *kākalī-Ni* are both used, we have the *śuddha-kākalī-antara mūrchanas* of nine notes.[24]

In this way we obtain, in both *grāmas*:

14 *śuddha mūrchanas* of seven notes

16 *śuddha-kākalī mūrchanas* of eight notes

16 *śuddha-antara mūrchanas* of eight notes

18 *śuddha-kākalī-antara mūrchanas* of nine notes

totaling sixty-four *mūrchanas* on which most of the modes (*rāgas*) are based.

Not all these *mūrchanas* are usable, nor are they all used in practice in modern music. Those most used are numbers 1, 2, 5, 6, 10, 12, and 14 of example 7—that is, generally, those in which the fifth and the fourth are perfect, though some have a large fourth (Ma+ [F+]). When comparing this classification with that of the Greeks, we shall see that if only the seven principal notes are used, the modes or *rāgas* can be called diatonic, while the introduction of the two accessory sounds allows the construction of chromatic scales.

Example 7. The fourteen *mūrchanas* of the *Sa* and *Ma Grāmas*
Mūrchanas of the *Sa grāma:*

7. Abhirudgata

Ga Ma MaL+ Pa Dha+ Ni Sa ReL+ Re Ga   Sa ReL+ (Re+) Ga♭ Ma+ Pa Dha♭ (Dha+) Ni♭ Sa

Mūrchanas of the *Ma grāma:*

8. Sauvīrī

Pa Dha Ni Sa ReL+ Re Ga Ma MaL+ Pa   Sa Re+ Ga Ma (MaL+) Pa Dha NiL+ (Ni+) Sa

9. Harināśvā

Ma MaL+ Pa Dha Ni Sa ReL+ Re Ga Ma   Sa (ReL+) Re Ga MaL+ Pa (Dha♭) Dha+ Ni Sa

10. Kalopanata

Ga Ma MaL+ Pa Dha Ni Sa ReL+ Re Ga   Sa ReL+ (Re+) Ga♭ Ma Pa Dha♭ (Dha++) Ni♭ Sa

11. Śuddha madhya

Re Ga Ma MaL+ Pa Dha Ni Sa ReL+ Re   Sa Re– GaL (Ga+) Ma Pa– Dha NiL+ (Ni+) Sa

12. Mārgī

Sa ReL+ Re Ga Ma MaL+ Pa Dha Ni Sa   Sa (ReL+) Re Ga Ma (MaL+) Pa Dha+ Ni Sa

13. Pauravī

Ni Sa ReL+ Re Ga Ma MaL+ Pa Dha Ni   Sa ReL+ (Re+) Ga♭ Ma MaL+ (Pa+) Dha♭ Ni♭ Sa

14. Harishyakā

Dha Ni Sa ReL+ Re Ga Ma MaL+ Pa Dha   Sa Re Ga♭ (Ga++) Ma+ Pa Dha♭ (Dha++) Ni♭ Sa

Among these scales we can note that the modern Western major mode corresponds to the *Mārgī mūrchana* of *Ma grāma* and not to the *Rajanī mūrchana* of *Sa grāma*, which contains A+ (Dha+).

When Śivendranatha, in his *Rāga-vibodha*, says for example that the *Pauravī* and *Uttarāyata mūrchanas* begin from Dha (A), he takes as a general tonic the medieval one, Re (D). This means that the pure (unaltered) scale is considered to be that of *Kāfī*, which contains, in relation to the tonic C (Sa), a flat E (Ga) and a flat B (Ni). We have chosen here to keep the modern unaltered scale, *Bilāval*, the major mode, as the pure scale. Therefore, the same *Pauravī* and *Uttarāyata* begin for us with a B (Ni). This does not in any way alter the order of the notes in these *mūrchanas*. The difference is merely one of conventional notation.

The scales made on the basis of tetrachords, which are directly obtained on the *vīna* and other stringed instruments, can be added to the *mūrchana* scales. Such scales generally have two identical tetrachords. Other scales are obtained by changing the *śruti* of the tonic; a certain number of them are described in the *Sangīta-ratnākara*.[25]

Chromatic and Enharmonic

If, leaving aside the details of tuning, we assemble the notes of the different *mūrchanas*, we get a chromatic scale that corresponds to the Western form of the scale (see example 8).

Example 8.

Sa	Re-k	Re	Ga-k	Ga	Ma	Ma-t	Pa	Dha-k	Dha	Ni-k	Ni	Sa
C	D♭	D	E♭	E	F	F♯	G	A♭	A	B♭	B	C

But if we are careful about precise tuning, we find that to transpose all the *mūrchanas* to the same pitch we require two distinct positions for each note, separated by an interval of one comma, giving the enharmonic scale:

$$\begin{array}{ccccccc}
 & \text{L-}\ \text{L+} & & & \text{L}\ \ \flat & & \\
\text{C} & \text{D}\flat\ \text{D}\flat & \text{D—D} & \text{E}\flat\ \text{E}\flat & \text{E E+} & \text{F F+} \\
\text{Sa} & \text{ReL- ReL+} & \text{Re— Re} & \text{GaL Ga}\flat & \text{Ga Ga+} & \text{Ma Ma+}
\end{array}$$

$$\begin{array}{ccccccc}
\text{L-}\ \text{L+} & & & \text{L}\ \ \flat & & \text{L-}\ \text{L+} & \\
\text{F♯ F♯} & \text{G G+} & \text{A}\flat\ \text{A}\flat & \text{A A+} & \text{B}\flat\ \text{B}\flat & \text{B B+} & \text{C} \\
\text{MaL- MaL+} & \text{Pa Pa+} & \text{DhaL Dha}\flat & \text{Dha Dha+} & \text{NiL- NiL+} & \text{Ni Ni+} & \text{Sa}
\end{array}$$

This series can be represented in Western notation as in example 9.

Example 9.

If we exclude from this series G+ (Pa+, A♭♭), because the fifth is invariable, we obtain a scale of twenty-two sounds, the *śrutis*, grouped in pairs, each pair forming an interval of one comma. According to Bhārata,[26] the method employed to obtain this scale consists in tuning two identical instruments (*vīnas*) in the *Sa grāma*. Then, by adapting one of them to the *Ma grāma* with the help of the difference between the perfect fourths E A (Ga Dha) and A+ D (Dha+ Re), as previously explained, the A+ (Dha+) is lowered by one comma to A (Dha). If we then keep this new A (Dha) as a fixed sound and retune the instrument in the *Sa grāma*, all the notes of this instrument will be one comma lower than those of the first instrument. The combined notes of the two instruments then give the scale of twenty-two *śrutis*.

This scale is identical to the one described by Arab mathematicians as that of the ancient Greeks, and it still remains the division used by the Arabs themselves. The major tone is thus divided into minor tone, apotome (or major half tone), and limma:

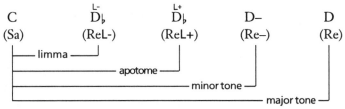

These twenty-two positions of the notes, or *śrutis*, are said to correspond to definite and distinct feelings. According to certain authors they can be further divided into sixty-six positions, so as to allow perfect consonance in every instance. But this is only a question of more or less perfect tuning, and the number of possible distinct feelings remains limited to twenty-two.

This division of the octave into twenty-two intervals has been considered arbitrary by modern Sanskritists and musicologists, who have written the most amusing abuses against it. Yet such a division is not only logical but essential. It is in reality used in every country and is valid for all music, from the point of view of acoustics as well as that of mathematics or metaphysics, and even from the point of view of musical expression, as we shall shortly see.

Acoustic Definition of the Division of Śrutis

After the elementary division of the octave into twelve half tones, which can be called the division of the first order, all acoustically acceptable divisions of the octave must necessarily take into account the difference between twelve fifths and seven octaves. This is called the Pythagorean comma, and is approximately equal to a fifty-third of an octave. Its harmonic equivalent, the comma *diesis*, is the difference between the major and minor tones. The simplest divisions are those that take the comma as a unit and can be called the divisions of the second order. The first division of the second order is obviously the complete division into fifty-three intervals. But in this division, if we keep only the most important values for each of the twelve notes, removing, twelve by twelve, those values that are less employed in practice, the fifty-three original notes are successively reduced to forty-one, then twenty-nine, and finally seventeen, which is the minimum division of the second order and is the basic division used by the Arabs.

But the fifty-third fifth, as we already saw in connection with Chinese music, again goes beyond the octave by a fraction smaller than the comma. If we take as a unit this fraction of a comma, we obtain the divisions of the third order. This complete system divides the octave into 358 intervals, which through elimination of the less important fifths, twelve by twelve, can be reduced to the minimum division of the third order, which is of twenty-two intervals. This is the division adopted by the Indians, for metaphysical as well as musical reasons. As we have seen, the Chinese division stands in between, as it uses the division of the second order up to its maximum (fifty-three fifths) and then, up to the sixtieth fifth, uses intervals of the third order.

These divisions can be pursued indefinitely into divisions of the fourth, fifth, nth order. But the Indians, although they showed by this division the extent of their knowledge of acoustics and mathematics, have been able to avoid abstract speculation and to stop at the intermediate division of twenty-two *śrutis*; this division alone is in perfect agreement with musical practice, since any further division would go beyond that which, in terms of sounds, is equivalent to the third dimension, and being therefore beyond the limits of this universe, could be of no interest as regards musical practice.

Symbolic Necessity of the Division into Twenty-two Śrutis

From the point of view of numbers, the division of the modal octave must necessarily be of twenty-two intervals. This division is not peculiar to music, but represents a universal law. Indeed, the relation of those twenty-two intervals with the seven notes of the scale is the only one that can give to music a complete and logical substructure. René Guénon explains:

> The number twenty-two is related to seven by the ratio 22/7, which is the approximate expression of the relation between the circle and its diameter, so these two numbers together represent the circle, which is considered as the most perfect shape by Dante as well as by the Pythagoreans (each division of each of the three worlds has this circular form). Besides, in twenty two are united the symbols of two of the "elementary movements" of Aristotelian physics: the *local movement*, represented by two, and that of *alteration*, represented by twenty, as Dante himself explains in his *Convito*.[27]

The symbolic correspondences of the number seven and the number twenty-two are so numerous that it is not possible to attempt to study them here. We shall simply note that, in accordance with this symbolism, the *vīna*, the sacred instrument of Indian music, is made of two spheres joined together by a straight axis on which seven strings are played over twenty-two frets; the Hebrew alphabet, whose role is so important in the Qabalah, has twenty-two letters and seven double letters; seven planets determine, by their orbits around the sun, the limits of the visible world, while twenty-two cosmic circles separate us from the metaphysical sun, the central eye that sees everything—circles that we shall have to cross before we can reach the final absorption into absolute knowledge.

The Arabic division of the octave into seventeen intervals is also based on considerations of symbolism connected with Muslim esotericism. This by no means excludes their physical reality. That the Arabs divide the octave into seventeen intervals does not imply that those intervals are bigger than the *śrutis*, as many Westerners have lightly considered. Those divisions refer necessarily to identical notes, in conformity with the needs of musical expression, because they are the representation of metaphysical realities corresponding to the very nature of sounds as well as of all other aspects of the three worlds. The seventeen notes of the Arabic octave can be identified with seventeen of the *śrutis*. The *śrutis* left out are those which are least employed, since, following the deterioration of the cycle, the scale of C (*Sa grāma*) is the only one employed in modal music. In the ancient law, Hebraic or Hindu, the numbers and *śrutis* of the lost *grāmas* (scales) are piously kept, but in the new law (Islam), they are left out of the general theory because they are so rarely used. This is what al-Fārābī explained: "the two cycles that we have established each contain twenty-two degrees; these are the totality of the notes that are used on the lute, some frequently, others more rarely. We shall deal only with the notes that are ordinarily used and that consequently are the more natural."[28] Elsewhere, speaking of the tuning of the Hūrāsān's *tunbur*, he says: "the scale of this instrument contains, in this tuning, thirty-two degrees, the doubled notes being ten in number."[29]

The number seventeen, which was considered inauspicious in ancient times in both the West and the East, has on the contrary sometimes been taken as representative of the new gospel, Christian or Islamic.

"The number seventeen can be divided in two ways: into ten and seven to represent the fusion of the ancient law and the new law (the law of fear is represented by the number ten, and the law of love by the number seven, says Saint Augustine); it can also be divided into eight and nine, and therefore signifies the union of angels and men."[30]

"One finds in the number seventeen . . . a wonderful mystery. It is not without reason that Psalm 17 is the only one to be found in the book of Kings, because it has for its subject the glory of the eternal kingdom in which we shall have no more enemies."[31]

On the other hand, Plutarch says: "the Pythagoreans . . . have for the number seventeen an absolute and sacred repulsion. This is in relation to the fact that between the square number sixteen and the rectangle number eighteen, which are the only plane numbers whose perimeters happen to be equal to their areas, comes the number seventeen, which interferes between these two numbers, separates them from each other, and divides their ratio, $1^1/_8$, into two unequal parts [9/8 = 18/17 x 17/16]."[32]

According to Hindu *Sānkhya* philosophy, the number seventeen represents the subtle body (*sūkshma śarīra*), which is composed of the five principles of the elements (*tanmātras*), the five senses of perception (*jñānendriyas*), the five organs of action (*karmendriyas*), intellect (*buddhi*, in which *ahamkāra*, the notion of individual "ego," is included), and mind (*manas*): 5 + 5 + 5 + 2 = 17. This subtle body remains in existence through all the forms of posthumous life, and is destroyed only at the time of final liberation (*moksha*), which means complete reabsorption into the First Principle (*Brahman*). The metaphysical doctrine (Pythagorean and Vedantic) considers the subtle body as mortal and even takes it as the fearful symbol of ultimate death, whereas the religious doctrines, to which Christianity and Islam belong, and which do not envisage the final stage of liberation (*moksha*) but take heaven (*svarga*) to be the ultimate end, consider the subtle body, which is then called the soul, as immortal. The number seventeen therefore becomes the glorious symbol of immortality.

The seventeen divisions of the octave are given by the Arab writers as shown in example 10.[33]

Example 10.

But in the tuning of instruments, particularly the *tunbur* of Hārāsān, the second string, using the same frets and tuned either on the second, D (Re); the minor third, E♭ (Ga♭); the fourth, F (Ma); the fifth, G (Pa); or the sixth, A+ (Dha+), according to mode required, gives all the missing notes to form the complete scale (ex. 11).

Example 11.

If we leave aside the modified fifth and octave, which are never used, this brings us back exactly to the Indian division.

We see therefore that, although the Arabs use only limmas and commas to establish their scale, they supplement the lack of the second form of certain flats and sharps by the superposition of several plagal forms. Although this leads to a somewhat different classification, it does not in practice create any difference from the Indian division.

Musical Definition of the Śrutis

Musical intervals can be accurately defined in two ways, either by numbers (string lengths, frequencies, etc.) or, with no less accuracy, by their psychological correspondences, such as the feelings and images they necessarily evoke in our minds. There is no sound without a meaning, assert the Vedantists. In the guise of sounds, it is only the manifested idea that we perceive, and it is therefore logical to conceive a theory of sounds based on the ideas represented by the sounds rather than on their numerical values. "We hold that it is quite possible to build a rational theory of music without the help of numbers," says Rāja S. M. Tagore.[34]

In spite of the extreme confusion resulting from the use of equal temperament, Westerners still appreciate, in singing, the difference between a brilliant timbre and a somber timbre given to what is apparently the same note. This difference corresponds in reality to a difference of pitch generally equal to one comma, a difference similar to that between the major and the minor tones. This means that, although our spoiled ears can no longer appreciate the difference in the pitch of the sound, we remain able to define a difference of interval by a difference of color or feeling, or by emotional correspondences.

Although the *śrutis* are defined in terms of lengths of strings in the *Natya-śāstra* and particularly in the *Sangīta-parijāta* of Ahobala, Indian theorists generally prefer to define intervals by their feeling rather than by numbers. They consider this system to be quite as accurate and more practical because, without any mechanical verification, it allows the gifted musician, who alone is expected to take interest in music theory, to know immediately the accurate interval from the feelings it evokes.

For example, if, hearing continuously the tonic C (Sa), we try to sing or play the major third E (Ga) with a peaceful and loving feeling, we shall obtain the harmonic third, E (Ga) = 5/4, corresponding to the *śruti Ratikā*. But if our feelings had been of energy, wonder or heroism, we would inevitably have sung the third of the scale of fifths, the ditone E+ (Ga+) = 81/64, corresponding to the *śruti Raudrī*.[35]

Similarly, the minor third E♭ (Ga komal) or the minor seventh B♭ (Ni komal), when corresponding to a sentiment of pity, *karunā rasa*, will be respectively Ė♭ (GaL) = 32/27 and B̤♭ (NiL+) = 16/9 (*Dayāvatī* and *Madantī* srutis), while the same two intervals, when corresponding to the sentiment of love (*sringāra rasa*) or of amusement (*hāsya rasa*) are respectively Ė♭ (Ga♭) = 6/5 and B̤♭ (Ni) = 9/5 (*Rañjanī* and *Rohinī* srutis).

The natural A (Dha) of the harmonic scale, A (Dha) = 5/3 = 222 savarts, is peaceful and happy (*Sandīpanī śruti*), but the A+ (Dha+) of the scale of fifths, A+ (Dha+) = 16/27 = 227 savarts, is immodest and irritating (*Ālāpinī śruti*), and so on.

The feeling of the *śrutis* depends exclusively on their position in relation to the tonic. An augmented sixth (Dha tīvra) or a diminished seventh (Ni komal), for example, have, if they belong to the same *śruti*, the same feeling. The ancient Sanskrit names of the *śrutis* allow one easily to remember their meaning, and consequently to sing or to play them accurately. Figure 11 gives a list of the *śrutis* according to the system of Śārngadeva.[36]

Further Subdivisions of the Śrutis

The *śrutis* are represented in practice by their characteristic notes, but they are, theoretically, regions of the octave. Within the limits of each *śruti* several positions may be possible, allowing an adjustment of the tuning of the notes according to the mode or *rāga* being played or sung. As long as the notes do not trespass beyond the limits of the *śruti*, their mood keeps the same characteristics. This mood will be clearer and stronger if, within those limits, that note is used which forms the most rational and simple ratio with the tonic. This leads to the use, within the twenty-two *śrutis*, of the fifty-three (and sometimes sixty-six) divisions of the octave, which allow the necessary adjustments of tuning according to the mode or the *rāga*.

The limits of the *śrutis* are strictly determinate, a fact that has induced the Indian physicists to differentiate carefully between the limma (256/243 = 22.63 savarts) and its complement within the minor tone (135/128 = 23.12 savarts; 256/243 x 135/128 = 10/9). Those two intervals, although almost equal, represent respectively one *śruti* and two *śrutis* according to a rule stated in Sanskrit treatises.[37] For example, the four *śrutis* of the major tone can be divided as follows:

A	A+	L- B♭		L+ B♭		B
(Dha)	(Dha+)	(NiL-)		(NiL+)		(Ni)
	81/80 x 25/24		81/80		256/243	
	135/128					
	2 *śrutis*		1 *śruti*		1 *śruti*	

Misinterpretations of the Śrutis

The "enharmonic" division of the octave into twenty-four quarter tones by the ancient Greeks as well as by Southern Indians seems to be the result either of the addition of two theoretical intervals, the modified fifth and octave (which are never employed and would not bring out a distinct feeling), or of a confu-

Figure 11. THE TWENTY-TWO ŚRUTIS

Ancient note		Name	Mood	Modern note
Ni	0	Kshobhinī	irresolute, agitated	C (Sa)
	1	Tīvra	intense, acute, poignant, dreadful	D♭ (ReL-) ^L-
k-Ni	2	Kumudvatī	white lotus, moonflower	D♭ (ReL+) ^L+
	3	Manda	slow, wicked, lazy, cold, apathetic	D– (Re–)
Sa	4	Chandovatī	the basis of harmony	D (Re)
	5	Dayāvatī	compassionate, tender	E♭ (GaL) ^L
	6	Rañjanī	pleasing, coloring, lustful	E♭ (Ga♭)
Re	7	Ratikā	pleasure, sexuality	E (Ga)
	8	Raudrī	burning, terrible, calamitous	E+ (Ga+)
Ga	9	Krodha	anger, wrath	F (Ma)
	10	Vajrikā	thundering, steel, diamond, severe, abusive	F+ (Ma+)
a-Ga	11	Prasārinī	diffusing, pervading, shy	F♯ (MaL-) ^L-
	12	Prītih	pleasure, love, delight	F♯ (MaL+) ^L+
Ma	13	Mārjanī	cleansing, adorning, excuse	G (Pa)
	14	Kshitih	forgiving, destructible, earth	A♭ (DhaL) ^L
	15	Rakta	red, impassioned, colored, playful	A♭ (Dha♭)
	16	Sandīpanī	stimulating, inflaming	A (Dha)
Pa	17	Ālāpinī	speaking, conversing	A+ (Dha+)
	18	Madantī	lust, spring, intoxication	B♭ (NiL+) ^L+
	19	Rohinī	adolescent girl, lightning, growing	B♭ (Ni♭)
Dha	20	Ramya	night, love, pleasure, rest, calm	B (Ni)
	21	Ugra	sharp, passionate, cruel, formidable, powerful	B+ (Ni+)
Ni	22	Kshobhinī	irresolute, agitated	C (Sa)

sion in traditional data. The double octave was the range that was necessary in ancient Indian and Greek music, as it still is in Arab and Turkish music today, to define the mode. This double octave was divided into twenty-four (twice twelve) regions assimilated to the signs of the zodiac, among which the seven notes move like the seven planets.

The śruti *is not a tempered interval.* Not all *śrutis* are equal, but their division suffices to allow the classification of all the notes that have a distinct significance and that are used in the definition of *rāgas*—in fact, of all possible musical modes. In reality, the division into twenty-two is the minimum division that allows a clear definition of the expressive characteristics of intervals.

The division of the tone into several intervals is necessary for accurate playing, and although it is easy for a well-trained ear to discern whether an interval is accurate, it is extremely difficult if not impossible to find out, without special instruments, in what proportion an interval is bigger or smaller than another. This difficulty is why Greek musicians, appreciating intervals by ear and noticing that they were using two or three intermediate positions in the tone, may have considered them, as the Indians did, to be approximately equal in practice.[38] Such an attitude is quite understandable, but to take this approximation for a mathematical reality and make complicated calculations and lengthy theories on this basis, and then to come to the conclusion that the ancient Greeks and Indians were enjoying peculiar intervals that have no appeal for other ears, is an absurdity. Like every practical division of the octave, the division of the *śrutis* is theoretically insufficient, but to believe it to be a tempered division is to lower the scientific knowledge of the Indians to the level of modern musical practice; it is also in absolute contradiction to the Sanskrit treatises. Therefore when J. Grosset, like many others, takes the *śrutis* to be equal divisions in his article in the *Encyclopédie de la musique et dictionnaire du Conservatoire*, and compares them with the Western tempered scale, enlisting for this purpose the help of a "professor of mathematics" and of endless logarithms, he may be performing prodigious mathematical exercises, but they have no connection whatsoever with the theory or the practice of the *śrutis*.

The term *śruti*, like the Greek *quarter tone*, refers to the displacement of a note by an interval smaller than a half tone in order to obtain a harmonically accurate interval. This has nothing to do with an equal temperament either by half tones or quarter tones, and such calculations as I have used above bear no relation to this. The school of Aristoxenes in the fourth century divided the tone into four "rigorously equal" quarter tones, but in reality this division was not considered as exact because Aristoxenes did admit in practice a certain "freedom of variation of the intervals," a certain "latitude" for each note.[39] This clearly annihilates the rigor of the definition and shows that this is in reality a simplified and approximate division, which replaces an accurate division as far as it can but in no way allows any precise calculations or observations to be made on its basis.

The importance of the comma, equal to 81/80 or 5 savarts, which is the difference between the major and minor tones, is such that it can easily seem to be equivalent to the minor half tone, 25/24 or 18 savarts. This has been noted by E. Clements in his *Introduction to the Study of Indian Music*: "The ancients held the erroneous opinion that these intervals (*śrutis*) were equal. Their system was, however, a convenient one for distinguishing between the major tone (four *śrutis*), the minor tone (three *śrutis*) and the semitone (two *śrutis*). By an interval of 'one *śruti*' they understood the comma 81/80."[40] Though oversimplified and patently biased, this view is not inaccurate.

Raouf Yekta Bey, in his study on Turkish music, writes:

> Oriental instrumentalists, who care only for the practice of their music, having noted that the interval of a major tone contains three notes and that the major tone is thus divided into four parts, have given the name of *quarter tone* to each one of these four parts. Europeans, who have heard this expression, have understood that Orientals divide the tone into four equal parts. But no Arab, Turkish, or Persian theorist has ever spoken of the division of the major tone into four equal parts. . . . In the interval G A+ [Pa Dha+], starting from G [Pa], we have:
>
> 1) 243/256 (limma) [G (Pa) A♭ (DhaL-)]
>
> 2) 2048/2187 (apotome) [G (Pa) A♭ (DhaL+)]
>
> 3) 59049/65536 (minor tone) [G (Pa) A (Dha)].
>
> The intervals obtained by this method certainly do not divide the tone into four equal parts.[41]

Nine centuries earlier, Avicenna (Abū 'Alī al-Husayn ibn 'Abd Allah ibn Sīnā) was already laughing at the theorists who believed that the limma was a mathematical half tone and that the *irka* was a quarter tone, and he explains the exact value of their ratios.[42]

Western Division of the Octave into Twenty-two Intervals

Westerners, always ready to criticize the so-called quarter tones of Eastern music, nevertheless themselves acknowledge within the octave twenty-one different tones, which they represent by distinct signs. Their notation is in fact based on the triple septenary of seven naturals, seven sharps, and seven flats. If the octave is added, this gives 3 x 7 + 1 = 22. The fact that in tempered tuning systems two notes may be represented by one in no way implies that they are really identical. Indeed, they are so far from being identical that, to indicate the same tempered note, two signs are maintained, which would be illogical if there were really only one sound.

This division differs only by one note from the Indian division. But not even noticing that their own notation implies twenty-one distinct sounds in the octave, no doubt too "civilized" to care for the elementary laws of physics and mathematics that necessitate such a division, Westerners often speak in contemptuous terms of musical systems other than their own, and describe Asian musicians as "like the Greeks, more intent in splitting tones into quarters and eighth parts, of which they compute the ratios to show their arithmetic, than on displaying the principles of modulation as it may affect the passions."[43]

Such regrettable views only show that these otherwise learned scholars are as unaware of the realities of musical practice in their own country as they are of the strong acoustic and mathematical grounds of the Eastern musical theory that they so lightly venture to ridicule. They do not seem to realize that the intervals used by Eastern musicians and by the great Western violinists are, for the impartial ear of sound-measuring instruments, generally identical, although the simplifications necessitated by their practical notation may sometimes hide this identity because it dissimulates the true nature of the component sounds. It is unfortunate that this deficiency regarding the knowledge of t'₂e elements of acoustic reality has not prevented many a Western scholar from writing books about scales.

Such an approach to purely scientific questions may be culturally most destructive because the musical systems concerned often belong to peoples who have passed through a period of political dependence when their culture was at the mercy of education officials who could open or close educational institutions at will, and who were, for music at least, obviously not qualified to form an independent opinion. Even after political independence, the cultural imperialism of the West continues to be extremely powerful. When an apparently unbiased scholar such as J. Grosset, who is generally considered in Western countries to be an authority, spoke of "this musical past . . . whose asserted splendor, if it ever existed, has for long been forgotten,"[44] and described the classification of notes as "those childish speculations, which do not deserve any attention except as a characteristic indication of Indian mentality,"[45] he may have inspired with all the weight of his authority the actions of officials who, in the name of civilization, did their best to destroy some of the most precious monuments and greatest treasures of human culture. Unfortunately, such utterances as these can do incalculable harm, for to the layman they are the opinions of experts, and the layman cannot be expected to know that these same experts are as ignorant as he is himself of the intricacies and significance of the things they speak of in such contemptuous and authoritative terms.

Influence of Indian Theory in Europe

It seems that some of the conceptions that are the basis of Indian theory were known in Europe at the end of the Middle Ages, indirectly by way of Egyptian and Pythagorean tradition transmitted to the Arabs and Byzantines. This indirect transmission can explain the numerous mistakes in the application of these principles to musical practice. The three scales, or *grāmas*, have become the three *hexacorda*:

Hexacordum naturale C D E F G A (Sa Re Ga Ma Pa Dha)

Hexacordum durum G A B C D E (Pa Dha Ni Sa Re Ga)

Hexacordum molle F G A B C D (Ma Pa Dha Ni Sa Re).

To the symbols of the Greek alphabetic notation of the scale, A, B, C, D, E, F, G, a, b, c, d, e, f, g, aa, are added five upper sounds and one lower sound, *gamma*, to give a scale of twenty-two sounds. The word *gamut* (French *gamme*, Latin *gamma*) singularly resembles the Sanskrit *grāma* (village) or Prākrit *gama*, though I am not qualified to decide whether this word comes from Greek or Sanskrit; the mere fact that in two different places the same word is used to represent the same thing is not a proof in itself.[46]

The Jātis

The twenty-two *śrutis* are divided into five families, or *jātis*, according to their mood. The different relations that can be established between these five families allow the classification of the notes in the different modes (*rāgas*) according to their mood.

Figure 12 shows the five *jātis* as they are defined in the *Sangīta-ratnākara* and the *Sangīta-parijāta*.

The *jātis* correspond not to scales but to similarities of expression. It is impossible to build a scale in which all the notes have a similar mood, that is, in which all the notes belong to the same *jāti*. Only when the scale has been built according to the general rules of proportion can one see whether its different notes incline toward a certain feeling—enter into a certain *jāti*—or not.

Figure 13 shows the twenty-two *śrutis* in sequence, with the *jātis* to which they belong. The classification of individual notes into *jātis* in this manner is known as *śruti-jāti*. The classification of scales according to the number of notes used in ascending and descending is known as *rāga-jāti*.

Affinities of the Musical Notes

As we have already seen, the different aspects of the perceptible world are parallel manifestations of undifferentiated common principles. Their development consequently follows parallel courses with similar divisions. There are

Figure 12. THE FIVE *JĀTIS*

Family	*rasa* (emotional flavor)	*śrutis*
Dīpta	marvelous	*Raudrī* E+ (Ga+)
(shining, illustrious)	heroic	*Vajrikā* F+ (Ma+)
	furious	*Ugra* B+ (Ni+)
		Tīvra D♭ (ReL-)
Mriduh	love	*Ratikā* E (Ga)
(soft)		*Prītih* F♯ (MaL+)
		Kshitih A♭ (DhaL)
		Manda D– (Re–)
Āyata	comic	*Krodhā* F (Ma)
(abundant)		*Prasārinī* F♯ (MaL-)
		Sandīpanī A (Dha)
		Rohinī B♭ (NiL+)
		Kumudvatī D♭ (ReL+)
Madhya	comic	*Chandovatī* D (Re)
(moderate)	love	*Rañjanī* E♭ (GaL)
		Mārjanī G (Pa)
		Rakta A♭ (Dha♭)
		Ramya B (Ni)
		Kshobhinī C (Sa)
Karunā	pathetic	*Dayāvatī* E♭ (GaL)
(compassionate)	odious	*Ālāpinī* A+ (Dha+)
	terrible	*Madantī* B♭ (NiL+)

Figure 13. THE ŚRUTIS AND THEIR EXPRESSIVE QUALITIES

Ancient Sa grāma		Śruti	Jāti	Rasa	Modern note	Interval
Ni	0	Kshobhinī			C (Sa)	
	1	Tīvra	Dīpta	marvelous, heroic, furious	D♭ (ReL-)	limma
k-Ni	2	Kumudvatī	Āyata	comic	D♭ (ReL+)	comma
	3	Manda	Mriduh	love	D- (Re-)	minor half tone
Sa	4	Chandovatī	Madhya	comic, love	D (Re)	comma
	5	Dayāvatī	Karunā	compassion	E♭ (GaL)	limma
	6	Rañjanī	Madhya	comic, love	E♭ (Ga♭)	comma
Re	7	Ratikā	Mriduh	love	E (Ga)	minor half tone
	8	Raudrī	Dīpta	marvelous, heroic, furious	E+ (Ga+)	comma
Ga	9	Krodha	Āyata	comic	F (Ma)	limma
	10	Vajrikā	Dīpta	marvelous, heroic, furious	F+ (Ma+)	comma
a-Ga	11	Prasārinī	Āyata	comic	F♯ (MaL-)	minor half tone
	12	Prītih	Mriduh	love	F♯ (MaL+)	comma
Ma	13	Mārjanī	Madhya	comic, love	G (Pa)	limma
	14	Kshitih	Mriduh	love	A♭ (DhaL)	limma
	15	Rakta	Madhya	comic, love	A♭ (Dha♭)	comma
	16	Sandīpanī	Āyata	comic	A (Dha)	minor half tone
Pa	17	Ālāpinī	Karunā	compassion	A+ (Dha+)	comma
	18	Madantī	Karunā	compassion	B♭ (NiL+)	limma
	19	Rohinī	Āyata	comic	B♭ (Ni♭)	comma
Dha	20	Ramya	Madhya	comic, love	B (Ni)	minor half tone
	21	Ugra	Dīpta	marvelous, heroic, furious	B+ (Ni+)	comma
Ni	22	Kshobhinī	Madhya	comic, love	C (Sa)	limma

therefore natural and irresistible correspondences between the different aspects of manifestation, and starting from one particular aspect one can easily reach or evoke the corresponding stages in the other aspects.

According to this principle, the notes and chords of music have exact equivalents in every category of existence. Only the knowledge of such correspondences can allow us to understand the real meaning of sounds and to use them rationally as a means of evocation.

We shall give here some of the principal correspondences indicated in the Sanskrit treatises. Such correspondences are always envisioned from the point of view of the geometry of sounds, and they are therefore equally valid for the modal degree and the polyphonic interval, which are simply two different applications of one relation. What is said here of the fifth degree G (Pa), for example, also applies to the fifth as a polyphonic interval.

In his *Sangīta-parijāta*, Ahobala says:

Sa [C], Ga [E♭], and Ma [F] are born from the family of *devas* [angels].

Pa [G] is born of ancestors, Re [D] and Dha [A] are born of the family of *munis* [sages], Ni [B♭] is born of the family of demons.[47] This is the distinction of families.

Sa [C], Ma [F], and Pa [G] are *brahmins* [priests]; Re [D] and Dha [A] are *kshatriyas* [warriors]; Ga [E] and Ni [B] are *vaiśyas* [traders]; the altered notes [sharps or flats (*tīvras* or *komals*)] are *śūdras* [laborers].

Thus the learned scholars have described the distinction of castes.

The note Sa [C] is like a lotus, Re [D] is of a reddish yellow, Ga [E] is like gold, Ma [F] is like jasmine.

Pa [G] is black, Dha [A] is yellow, and Ni [B♭] is variegated. Such are the colors of the notes.

There are seven continents: Jambu, Śaka, Kuśa, Krauñcha, Śālmalī, Śveta, and Pushkara. The seven notes are born respectively from the seven continents.

Agni [the fire deity], Brahmā, Mrigānka [the moon], Vishnu, the sage Nārada [the celestial singer], Tumburu, and Kuvera [the god of wealth] are respectively the seers of the seven notes. [To "see the notes" means to have direct knowledge of their absolute pitch.]

Vahni [fire], Brahmā, Sarasvati [goddess of learning], Sarva [Śiva], Sri [Lakshmī], Ganeśa, and the sun are the respective gods of the seven notes. . . .

Sa [C] and Ma [F] are in comic mood; Dha [A] and Ni [B♭] in erotic mood; Pa [G] in odious, pathetic, and terrible mood; Re [D] in erotic mood; Ga [E♭] in comic mood.

Tīvra [sharp] is in heroic, marvelous, and horrible mood, *tīvratara* [sharpened by two *śrutis*] is in comic mood, and even *tīvratama-Ma* [Ma sharpened by three *śrutis*, i.e., Pa– (G–)] is in erotic mood; . . . *mridu-Ma* [Ma– (F–)] is in comic mood. Thus is truly the distinction of the moods [*rasas*] of the seven notes. Here ends the description of notes.[48]

There are several systems of correspondences between notes and planets, angels, gods, colors, castes, seasons, emotions (*rasas*), and so on; at first sight these can appear contradictory, but in reality they refer to different fundamental (*śuddha*) scales. These systems are studied in detail in my book *The Rāgas of Northern Indian Music*. We should only note here that the names of animals attributed to the notes in the tradition of the *Sāmaveda* are in the same order as those used by medieval and modern authors, but transposed. Thus the cry of the peacock, which represents Pa (G) in the *Sāmaveda*, now corresponds to Sa (C). If, as is asserted by Indian musicians, the cry of these animals is always at the same pitch, this would indicate that standard pitch has risen by one fourth since Vedic times.

The Chinese, who attach great importance to the exactitude of their standard pitch, have to this day kept this primitive pitch, which is also that of the *yekah*, or tonic, in Arabic music. The *mesa* of ancient Greek music had, according to the calculations of Gevaert, the same pitch as the modern Western F♯, which, if we take into account the difference of one half tone existing between the usual Indian pitch and modern Western standard pitch, brings us again to the same note.

The Modes or Rāgas

The term *rāga* is much more accurate than the term *mode* as usually understood in the West. *Rāga* ("passion") denotes a group of sounds used for the representation of a definite emotional state. Another element of Western music that has something in common with the *rāga* is the figured bass, which leaves every possibility open for variation but defines the expressive outline in advance.

Insisting upon only one form of emotion, the mood slowly penetrates even the most inattentive hearers and establishes itself in their minds. That is why the power of suggestion of modes and *rāgas* is so much stronger than that of other musical forms, in which the mood is always changing. This influence can be strong enough to bring about physical and psychological transformations that seem unbelievable to those who are accustomed only to the powerful but relatively superficial effects of harmonic music.

Like all ancient peoples, the Greeks attached great importance to the power of modes as a means of imposing upon the mind certain conceptions and points of view. Their value as instruments of education, or means of influencing the masses, was therefore recognized, and their use regulated.

According to Aristotle:

> Some modes, such as the Mixolydian, incline people toward melancholy, toward more concentrated feelings. Others, such as the relaxed modes, inspire carelessness and laziness. Another intermediary harmony brings calm and peace to the soul; only the Dorian mode can produce this effect,

while the Phrygian mode stimulates enthusiasm. . . . All hymns conse-
crated to Bacchus, and all such movements, take their particular character
from their adaptation to the Phrygian mode; such is also the case for the
dithyramb, which is considered by all as a Phrygian invention. . . . As for
the Dorian harmony, all are unanimous in recognizing its character of
constant gravity and male firmness. . . . To it can be added other similar
modes that are adequate for the education of children because they are, at
the same time, able to instruct them and to raise in them the notion of
decency.[49]

Definition of Rāgas

A mode, or *rāga*, is defined by four indispensable factors:

1) A *tonic*, constantly played, upon which the whole modal structure depends.

2) A *scale*, containing between five and nine notes. Melodies that make use of
more than nine notes are mixtures of modes, and compositions of less
than five notes are only "melodic figures" (*tāna*). There is generally a
difference between the ascending (*āroha*) and descending (*avāroha*) forms
of the scale.

3) Certain *melodic figures*, and ways of attacking the notes, which are called
the form (*rūpa*) of the mode. They constitute the "theme."

4) A *dominant*. In each mode, a note—not necessarily the tonic, though in
some cases it may be—is played more often than the others, is always
accentuated, and is dwelt on for a longer time. This note is called *vādī*
(that which speaks). It is said to be the *rāja* (king) of the melody. A second
note, of almost equal importance, is called *samvādī* (consonant); it is either
a fourth or a fifth above the *vādī*. The other notes of the mode are called
anuvādī (assonant). The notes that do not belong to the mode are called
vivādī (dissonant).

These four elements—the tonic, the scale, the shape imposed by the *rūpa*,
and the dominant note—are sufficient to determine a mode and its feeling.
Within these limits all combinations of rhythms and melodies are allowed, but
the slightest use of a *vivādī* note, or of melodic figures belonging to the *rūpa* of
another mode, spoils the atmosphere and mood of a *rāga*.

If the four elements of a *rāga* are known, the *rāga* is perfectly determined,
but if one of those elements is missing, the *rāga* remains indeterminate and it
is impossible to define its meaning or expression. This is also the case, for
example, with Gregorian plainchant, where the tonic is always uncertain.

The classical treatises generally describe seventy-two principal *rāgas*, to
which are added derived *rāgas* reaching a total of several hundred. This is only
the number of *rāgas* actually in use, because the number of theoretically possible
rāgas is much greater. Ahobala speaks of 13,726,560 different combinations of

notes and of 18,678 *rāgas* of seven notes, 31,050 *rāgas* of six notes, and 17,505 *rāgas* of five notes in the *Ma grāma* alone.

The Periods of the Day

Much importance is attached in Indian music to the connection between *rāgas* and the periods of the day. Westerners recognize that certain musical works can represent morning, midday, or night, but they have never tried to define the intervals by which they are characterized, and they find it quite natural to play them at any hour. Indians do not approve of such a lack of sensitivity; *rāgas* of the night should be played at night, and those of the dawn at dawn. Only then can we fully understand and enjoy them without effort, because we ourselves change according to the hour, and the day in its brief cycle is the image of life.

Played at times other than those which they represent, *rāgas* can for a moment change the course of nature; musicians playing the *ragas* of night during the day, for example, have been seen to appear gradually surrounded by intense darkness. This connection of *rāgas* with the hours of the day is also known to the Persians and Arabs, but their calculation is not as precise as that of the Indians.

There are three main divisions of the day:

1. The day, of which the sun is the luminary
2. The night, of which the moon is the luminary
3. The twilight, of which fire is the luminary

The sun is said to have 116 rays, the moon 136, and fire 108. Their sum is equal to 116 + 136 + 108 = 360. To this corresponds the division of the day into 360 units of four minutes each. Six of these units form one *ghatikā* of twenty-four minutes, of which there are sixty in twenty-four hours. These have been connected with the division of the octave into commas. Twelve of these small units form one *muhūrt*, of forty-eight minutes, of which there are thirty in a day, each of them being dedicated to a particular deity. The day is further divided into eight watches (*praharas*) of three hours each and, further, into twenty-four hours (twice twelve), assimilated to the twelve regions of the octave, the signs of the zodiac, and so on. The day and the night comprise an ascending part, of masculine character, and a descending part, of feminine character, because "manifestation or growth is masculine, disappearance or decline is feminine, and neuter is the intermediate condition."[50] All these elements have their importance in determining the proper time to play the different *rāgas*, principally regulated by the respective value of the notes in regard to sun, moon, and fire. The main divisions are therefore:

1) *Sandhiprakāśa rāgas*, for the conjunction of the day and night (sunset and sunrise), whose general characteristics are Re komal (D♭) and Ga tīvra (E natural)

2) After *Sandhiprakāśa* (first part of the day or night), usually characterized by Re (D), Ga (E) and Dha śuddha (A natural)

3) Before *Sandhiprakāśa* (second part of day and night), characterized by Ga komal (E♭) and Ni komal (B♭)

These periods are further defined by the following particularities:

1. Between midday and midnight the *vādī* (dominant note) is in the lower tetrachord (*pūrvāṅga*), i.e., between Sa (C) and Ma (F).

2. Between midnight and midday the *vādī* is in the upper tetrachord (*uttarāṅga*), from Pa (G) to Sa (C).

3. The augmented fourth, Ma tīvra (F♯), belongs to the critical times of midday and midnight, sunrise and sunset, solstices and equinoxes. It may also exist in the morning, but then it is dominated by Ga komal (E♭). There are some exceptions to this rule, when Ma tīvra (F♯) corresponds to an expression of fear and pain.[51]

4. In the defective modes of six or five notes, the evening modes never leave out Ga (E) and Ni (B) (*udātta* notes), and the morning modes never leave out Re (D) and Dha (A) (*anudātta* notes).

The Modal or Harmonic Division of the Octave

Indian *deśī* music is essentially modal, which means that the intervals on which the musical structure is built are calculated in relation to a permanent tonic. This does not mean that the relations between sounds other than the tonic are not considered, but that each note will be established first according to its relation to the fixed tonic and not, as in the case of the cycle of fifths, by any permutation of the basic note. The modal structure can thus be compared to the proportional division of a straight line rather than to the periodic movement of a spiral. According to the symbolism of numbers, these proportional divisions are connected with certain ideas, forms, and emotions.

The object of harmonic science is to classify these proportions according to their symbolism and the feelings, images, or symbols they express. Only on this basis can modes be logically constructed and their expression precisely defined. All the notes obtained in the harmonic system are distinct from those of the cyclic system, which is based on different data. Yet though the notes are theoretically distinct and their sequence follows completely different rules, in practice they lead to a similar division of the octave into fifty-three intervals.

Figure 14 shows the scale of proportions, which is the basis of all modal music.[52] This scale is made of a succession of commas (81/80 = 5 savarts), with disjunctions of eight savarts. The disjunctions can be divided into two equal parts by an intermediate sound, which corresponds to the quarter tone. In the same table, we show the place of the twenty-two *śrutis*, according to the definitions of the ancient treatises, corroborated by the practice of present-day traditional musicians.

Figure 14. DIVISION OF THE OCTAVE INTO FIFTY-THREE INTERVALS AND TWENTY-TWO ŚRUTIS

Harmonic division	0	1	2		3	4	5	6		7	8	9
Modern scale	C Sa	+	++	¼	#	L-	L+	♭	¾	—	–	D Re
Relation to tonic		81/80	46/45	31/30	25/24	256/243	16/15	27/25	135/124	11/10	10/9	9/8
Interval		comma	comma	disjunction		comma	comma	comma	disjunction		comma	comma
Ancient scale	Ni						k-Ni					Sa
Śruti	0				1	2					3	4

Harmonic division	9	10	11		12	13	14		15	16	17
Modern scale	D Re	+	++	¼	#	L	♭	¾	—	–	E Ga
Relation to tonic	9/8	256/225	15/13	93/80	75/64	32/27	6/5	75/62	128/105	100/81	5/4
Interval		comma	comma	disjunction		comma	comma	disjunction		comma	comma
Ancient scale	Sa										Re
Śruti	4				5	6					7

Harmonic division	17	18	19		20	21	22
Modern scale	E Ga	+	++	¼	—	–	F Ma
Relation to tonic	5/4	81/64	32/25	31/24	125/96	320/243	4/3
Interval		comma	comma	disjunction		comma	comma
Ancient scale	Re						Ga
Śruti	7	8					9

Harmonic division	22	23	24		25	26	27	28		29	30	31
Modern scale	F Ma	+	++	¼	#	L-	L+	♭	¾	—	–	G Pa
Relation to tonic	4/3	27/20	512/375	62/45	25/18	45/32	64/45	36/25	90/62	375/256	40/27	3/2
Interval		comma	comma	disjunction		comma	comma	comma	disjunction		comma	comma
Ancient scale	Ga						a-Ga					Ma
Śruti	9	10				11	12					13

Harmonic division	31	32	33		34	35	36		37	38	39
Modern scale	G Pa	+	++	¼	♯	L	♭	¾	—	–	A– Dha
Relation to tonic	3/2	243/160	192/125	31/20	25/16	128/81	8/5	50/31	81/50	400/243	5/3
Interval		comma	comma	disjunction		comma	comma	disjunction		comma	comma
Ancient scale	Ma										Pa
Śruti	13					14	15				16

Harmonic division	39	40	41		42	43	44	45		46	47	48
Modern scale	A Dha	+	++	¼	♯	L-	L+	♭	¾	—	–	B Ni
Relation to tonic	5/3	27/16	128/75	31/18	125/72	225/128	16/9	9/5	29/16	11/6	50/27	15/8
Interval		comma	comma	disjunction		comma	comma	comma	disjunction		comma	comma
Ancient scale	Pa											Dha
Śruti	16	17					18	19				20

Harmonic division	48	49	50		51	52	53
Modern scale	B Ni	+	++	¼	—	–	C Sa
Relation to tonic	15/8	243/128	48/25	31/16	125/64	160/81	2/1
Interval		comma	comma	disjunction		comma	comma
Ancient scale	Dha						Ni
Śruti	20	21					22

~ *Chapter Six* ~

CONFUSION OF THE SYSTEMS: THE MUSIC OF THE GREEKS

Because analogy is the law of all things . . . things in
this world could not be independent; indeed, of neces-
sity, there had to be a certain relation between them.

Plotinus, *Third Aeneid*, II, 18

There seems to be in the nature of harmony and rhythm
something similar to human nature. Therefore, some
philosophers assert that the soul is a harmony.

Aristotle, *Politics*, V, 4, 7

Ancient Greek Music

If we try to study ancient Greek music from the point of view of Western scholarship, it is extremely puzzling. A great number of ill-assorted intervals seem to be assembled in genera and modes that appear strange and poorly adapted to the necessities of both acoustics and art. In addition, the genera, modes, or intervals are represented by ratios that, although mathematically very precise, differ from one theorist to another. When such laxity in definition is possible, so much precision in the measurement of the intervals seems rather arbitrary.

If, however, we consider the peculiar position of ancient Greek civilization, it is easy to find the key to this enigma. But first we shall have to repudiate the legend that the Greeks invented everything. Far from having invented anything in music, the Greeks received all the elements of their musical system from Egypt and the Near East, a fact that they never attempted to conceal. Where they really showed their originality was in their physicists' attempts to explain the laws of that music with the help of a theory that they had received from another source, and that in reality was applicable to another system. Since the physicists' theory could never coincide with the system as used by the musicians, many compromises had to be invented. This explains the multiplicity of combinations and ratios proposed for each mode according to the inventiveness of the physicists.

Greek music as it was actually played, being modal, is necessarily included in the definitions of ancient Indian music, because those definitions cover all the possibilities of modal music. Greek music, like Egyptian music, most probably had its roots in Indian music, or at least in that universal system of modal music of which the tradition has been fully kept only by the Indians. In opposition to this modal system, the cyclic system of the Greek physicists, based on the properties of numbers according to the doctrines of Pythagoras, is represented in its most complete form by Chinese musical theory.

As usual, the Greek physicists, the "scientists" unable to realize the limits of their own knowledge, accused the musicians of being ignorant and obstinate. Like all reformers, they considered as normal the stage of development reached in their time by the art they pretended to explain and improve, and they would have been most astonished had they been able to realize that any music built according to the logic of their theories would have been of quite a different nature and would have had little resemblance to the art that they loved. Such a music—Chinese music, for example—would have hurt their ears, and they certainly would have rejected it as "barbarous."

This is what was observed by the Arabs. "When, under the rule of the Abbasid caliphs, the Arabs came into direct contact with the Persian and Byzantine populations, their artists soon realized the very great differences that existed between the teachings of Greek theorists and the art practiced by those populations—that living and real art which, more than scholarly works could do, has imprinted upon Arab music a mark of which there still remain deep traces today."[1]

This conflict of theories gives rise to so much confusion that ancient Greek music would not be a subject of particular interest for the study of scales (since we can study, in their complete form in China and India, the very systems from which it originated) if Western music had not inherited from Greece its ambiguous position between two systems and its inadequate theory, in addition to certain classifications. Because of the extravagant fanaticism with which the most arbitrary theories are so often imposed upon the whole world in the name of civilization, simply because they came from Europe, such theoretical confusions cannot be too strongly opposed, since under the guise of reforms and progress they undermine the basis of non-European musical systems that are most logically and solidly established.

We can get only a very faint idea of what ancient Greek music really was from the prejudiced explanations of theorists. Often we can get better data about technique and musical expression from the criticisms made of musicians than from the explanations of theorists, for these criticisms allow comparisons to be made with modal systems still in existence today. For example, the much-criticized habit of "pulling the strings" indicates the use of the *glissando* between the notes, just as in Indian music. Through this technique, a good musician can draw the most wonderful arabesques but in the hands of a lesser artist, they can become merely a kind of formless twittering in which the poorer musicians of India or of ancient Greece endlessly delight.

To study old Greek music we must be somewhat cautious about Greek theorists, but we must above all fear the works of modern Westerners because, as Raouf Yekta Bey has remarked humorously, "the writings of Europeans on ancient Greek music are so filled with errors and baseless hypotheses that, if we had to refute all of them, five volumes of encyclopedic size would not suffice."[2]

Besides, Europeans have no right to the title of sole heirs to and authorized commentators on ancient Greek music. In reality, the Arabs and the Turks happened to receive directly the inheritance of Greece. In many cases the works of Greek philosophers and mathematicians reached Europe through the Arabs. The most serious studies on Greek music were written by Arab scholars such as al-Fārābī in the tenth century and Avicenna a little later, while Westerners—Boethius in particular—had already made the most terrible mistakes. It is the Arabs who maintained a musical practice in conformity with this theory, a practice and theory that are still those of Arab music today. It would therefore seem elementary for Western scholars to take into account the interpretation of ancient Greek theory given by the Arabs before starting the fantastic reconstructions that have so prolifically flourished in Europe in recent years. Such a comparison is all the more necessary because the differences of interpretation concern the most fundamental definitions.

We are not in a position as yet to start the kind of detailed comparative study that would be necessary for any practical description of ancient Greek modes and the technical details necessary for their execution. Therefore, instead of presenting them, as is commonly done, as vague atonal scales absolutely insufficient for musical expression, we shall have to limit ourselves in this brief study to an attempt to outline in broad terms what is generally known of Pythagorean theory, its approximate application to modes, and the musical classifications of the Greeks.

As we have seen in connection with Indian *rāgas*, three elements at least are necessary for the definition of a mode, just as three notes are needed to define a chord. In the case of modes, these elements are the scale, the tonic (which is constantly present), and the dominant notes, which can be one or two in number (the *vādī* and *samvādī* of Indian music). The position of the mobile notes between the fixed tonic and dominant produces exactly the same numerical relationship, as do chords. But whereas in modulating systems, where every sound is mobile, it is necessary to repeat with each note the "body of harmony" (tonic, fifth or fourth, and octave) in order to establish the meaning or mood of the note, in the modal system one note alone, by changing its place, can produce the effect of a major or minor chord, in any inversion, a seventh chord, and so on. The modal frame, being fixed and firmly established in the memory of the hearer through the prelude, no longer needs to be constantly repeated, as do the chords of harmonic music, and it can sometimes even be left entirely implicit and understood.

Probably because of the commentators' ignorance of modal music, the three elements without which a mode cannot be defined do not appear clearly in any transcription of Greek modes. These studies should probably be redone, bearing in mind the particularities of modal systems, instead of trying to find the principles of harmony in the Greek modes at any cost.

The Theory of the Scale

The Pythagorean theory can be very briefly expressed as follows: "The demiurge has divided the composition [of the soul of the world] into seven parts, which relate to one another like the terms of two geometrical progressions, one of ratio 2 (1, 2, 4, 8) and the second of ratio 3 (1, 3, 9, 27). With the help of these two progressions, the demiurge has formed a single progression [of] 1, 2, 3, 4, 9, 8, 27."[3]

This Pythagorean progression, with its characteristic inversion of the fifth and sixth numbers, is to be found in every traditional system and is, for example, the basis of the scale on which the *Sāmaveda* is sung, a scale that in much more ancient times showed the same inversion.

The *Nārada-śikṣā* gives the Vedic scale (descending) as corresponding in classical Sanskrit notation to:

Ma	Ga	Re	Sa	Dha	Ni	Pa
(F)	(E♭)	(D)	(C)	(A)	(B♭)	(G)

or, in modern notation, to:

Pa	Ma	Ga	Re	Ni	Sa	Dha
(G)	(F)	(E)	(D)	(B)	(C)	(A)

The numbers representing these notes would correspond to those of the Pythagorean progression.

If we compare the numbers of these progressions two by two, we find six intervals and twelve relations:

1/2–2/1, 2/3–3/2, 3/4–4/3, 4/9–9/4, 9/8–8/9, 8/27–27/8

> The harmonic problem, according to the last passage of the *Republic*, consists in "unifying" the intervals, in filling the spaces between them with other terms that will form definite ratios with the first ones. This operation is called "harmonizing" (*harmonein*). . . . The result is the consonance (*sumphonia*) of intervals or their accord . . .
>
> Plato will thus fill the intervals of the primitive series 1 : 2 : 3 : 4 : 9 : 8 : 27 so as to find the musical intervals and their divisions.[4]

To fill the first interval, 1-2, he chooses, among the ratios formed by the terms of the series, the harmonic medium division (3/2) and the arithmetic medium division (4/3), whose relation (9/8) is divided into two unequal parts: the limma (256/243) and the apotome (2187/2048). The limma is the difference between two tones (81/64) and one fourth (4/3), and the apotome the difference between the limma and the tone (256/243 x 2187/2048 = 9/8).

In this way one obtains the following series:

1   9/8   81/64   4/3   3/2   27/16   243/128   2

In ancient Greece, the sounds that we call high were called low, so the numerical ratios were used in the opposite order. Interpreted according to modern ideas, that is, in ascending order, this numerical scale would give:

C	D	E+	F	G	A+	B+	C
(Sa)	(Re)	(Ga+)	(Ma)	(Pa)	(Dha+)	(Ni+)	(Sa)
1	9/8	81/64	4/3	3/2	27/16	243/128	2

intervals:	9/8	9/8	256/243	9/8	9/8	9/8	256/243
	major tone	major tone	limma	major tone	major tone	major tone	limma
savarts:	51	51	23	51	51	51	23

In this way we obtain two equal tetrachords, each containing two major tones and one limma, separated by a major tone (ex. 12).

This scale is identical to the scale of fifths, if we take as tonic the F (Ma), but if the tonic is kept as C (Sa), we find in it the arithmetic mean, 4/3 = F (Ma), instead of the seventh fifth, F♯ (Ma tīvra) = 512/729.

Example 12.

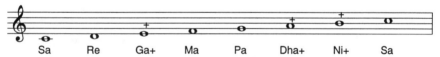

Sa   Re   Ga+   Ma   Pa   Dha+   Ni+   Sa

This is, in the Pythagorean system, the equivalent of the Western major scale or the Indian *Bilāval that*.

According to Indian theory, this interpretation of the Pythagorean scale should be correct for our times, as it corresponds to the current cosmic data. But in other periods, another interpretation must be given to it. This leads to somewhat different basic scales. The fact that the numerical Pythagorean scale can adapt itself to these different interpretations in accordance with the peculiarities of cosmic periods speaks in favor of the accuracy of the data on which it is based.

Starting from the higher C (Sa), that is, using the half-string as a unit, we must divide by two the numbers of the Pythagorean series to obtain the proportions on the full string.

The string lengths therefore become:

1/2   9/16   81/128   2/3   3/4   27/32   243/256   1

These give the following frequency ratios:

	L+	L			L	L-	
C	B♭	A♭	G	F	E♭	D♭	C
(Sa)	(NiL+)	(DhaL)	(Pa)	(Ma)	(GaL)	(ReL-)	(Sa)
1	16/9	128/81	3/2	4/3	32/27	256/243	1

intervals:	9/8	9/8	256/243	9/8	9/8	9/8	256/243
	major tone	major tone	limma	major tone	major tone	major tone	limma

savarts:	51	51	23	51	51	51	23

This scale is exactly the opposite of the former one. It is also exclusively composed of major tones and limmas, but being a descending scale it has its half tone at the lower end of each tetrachord. Examples 13 and 14 show two ways of notating this scale, which is called the Dorian mode, "the diatonic of the physicists," and which corresponds to the Indian *Bhairavī that.*

Example 13.

Sa   Ni L+   DhaL   Pa   Ma   Ga L   Re L−   Sa

Example 14.

Ga+   Re   Sa   Ni+   Dha+   Pa   Ma   Ga+

Genus

According to modern conceptions, a scale or mode is defined by the respective place occupied by the notes within the interval of one octave. For the ancient Greeks, however, it was otherwise, as it still is today for the Arabs: the relative place of the mobile notes within the fixed frame of the tetrachords defines genus and mode. "*Genus est certa quaedam tetrachordi divisio,*" wrote Aristides Quintilianus in his *De musica.* For the modal definition to be complete, four tetrachords are required, which have a different function though they are generally similar. This is why, in ancient Greek music, transposing a melody one octave higher changes its character, while a transposition of two octaves will bring back the same feeling.

The frame of the tetrachords is fixed and is formed by the tonic, the fourth, the fifth, and the octave. These are invariable and are called by Aristotle the "body of harmony." But within the tetrachords, the two other notes are mobile and, according to their position, form the enharmonic, chromatic, and diatonic genera. This classification is somewhat artificial and has given rise to the most amusing mistakes in interpretation and to the most violent invectives, which are certainly not justified.

The four tetrachords are the lower (I), the middle (II), the disjunct (III), and the upper (IV). To these four tetrachords must be added a lower note, the *proslambanomenos*, and a fifth tetrachord similar to the others but ending downward on the *mesa*, and called the conjunct tetrachord (V). In the diatonic genus, all these tetrachords formed the scale of the Pythagorean great perfect system, within whose frame the two groups of national (Dorian) and barbarian (Phrygian) harmonies developed.

These five tetrachords gravitate around the *mesa*, the highest note of the middle tetrachord, which was dedicated to the sun because it was the center of the whole musical system—the permanent note, constantly heard and in relation to which all other notes had significance. Western scholars interpret this scale as shown in example 15. But Safiyu-d-Dīn, as interpreted by d'Erlanger, gives the definition of the scale shown in figure 15 (to which we have added the corresponding Indian notations).

Example 15.

mesa   proslambomenos

Dha Pa Ma Ga Re Sa Ni Dha Pa Ma Ga Re Sa Ni (Dha) Re Sa Ni-k Dha

The different genera and modes found in ancient Greek music are still in use in Indian music today, although under an apparently different classification. But this classification, more convenient in practice for musicians, requires some experience of music and is therefore less easily handled by scholars. There are two classifications of sounds because sounds have two aspects, a physical aspect and an intellectual one. The physical aspect, the "form," is a material vibration that can be known by measurements or numbers, while the intellectual aspect, the "meaning" or expression, is directly perceived. Indians prefer to study musical sounds under this latter aspect only. They consider this system to be more practical because it can always be accurately established without the help of any measuring instrument.

According to Western scholars, the diatonic division of the scale was not the most ancient in Greece. It would be more accurate to say that it was not the basic definition. In spite of all the efforts of philosophers and mathematicians, it could never, in musical practice, replace the ancient enharmonic conception of the scale. An enharmonic notation always remained in use even for the diatonic scale. In reality, as we have already seen in Indian music, there can be no opposition or anteriority between the enharmonic scale (*śrutis*) and the diatonic scale (*grāmas*) since they necessarily coexist as two forms of the same thing. Because Western scholars have not meditated upon acoustics, and because of their undoubted tendency to assume that ancient theories are as arbitrary as their own, contradictions are seen where there is only a difference of approach.

Figure 15. THE PYTHAGOREAN GREAT PERFECT SYSTEM

Arabic scale	Ancient Indian scale	Modern scale	Arabic designation	Greek designation
G (Pa)	Ma	C (Sa)	Lowest given	Nete hyperboleon
A (Dha)	Pa	D (Re)	Lowest of the principal tetrachord	Paranete hyperboleon
B (Ni)	Dha	E (Ga)	Medium of the principal tetrachord	Trite hyperboleon
C (Sa)	Ni	F (Ma)	Highest of the principal tetrachord	Nete diezengmenon
D (Re)	Sa	G (Pa)	Lowest of the medium tetrachord	Paranete diezengmenon
E (Ga)	Re	A (Dha)	Medium of the medium tetrachord	Trite diezengmenon
F (Ma)	Ga	B♭ (Ni-komal)	Highest of the medium tetrachord	Paramesa
G (Pa)	Ma	C (Sa)	Central sound	Mesa
A (Dha)	Pa	D (Re)	Disjunctive of the central sound	Lichanos meson
B (Ni)	Dha	E (Ga)	Lowest of the disjunct tetrachord	Parypate meson
C♯ (Sa-tīvra)	kākali-Ni	F♯ (Ma-tīvra)	Medium of the disjunct tetrachord	Mese meson
D (Re)	Sa	G (Pa)	Highest of the disjunct tetrachord	Lichanos hypaton
E (Ga)	Re	A (Dha)	Lowest of the highest tetrachord	Parypate hypaton
F♯ (Ma-tīvra)	antara-Ga	B (Ni)	Medium of the highest tetrachord	Hypate hypaton
G (Pa)	Ma	C (Sa)	Highest of the highest tetrachord	Proslambanomenos

According to Maurice Emmanuel,

> The graphic system used by the Greeks to represent musical sounds is in formal contradiction with the Pythagorean division of the octave, which is based on tuning by means of fifths: it is called the vulgar or vocal diatonic. It is true that professional musicians and *dilettanti* partly accepted the Pythagorean construction. The fixed sounds, the "body of harmony," were placed in their true place with the help of the consonance of fifths according to the process already seen. Starting from the *mesa* the three other fixed sounds were obtained:

[Dha   Ga   Ni   Ga   Ni   Dha   Ga]

> But within this rigid frame they attempted to insert mobile sounds not arising from the fifths; these were therefore placed according to intervals smaller than half tones or bigger than tones.[5]

What were these contemptible intervals, which, without regard for twentieth-century decency, the Greeks inserted into the tetrachords, and against which Maurice Emmanuel felt all the more indignant because, according to him, they had "so regrettably succeeded"?

The Greeks divided musical modes into three genera:

1) The *diatonic*, in which each tetrachord is divided into two tones and one half tone

2) The *chromatic*, characterized in each tetrachord by a trihemitone, or minor third, the remaining tone usually being divided into two half tones

3) The *enharmonic*, whose characteristic interval is, in each tetrachord, a major third, or ditone, the remaining half tone usually being divided into two *dieses*, or quarter tones

Western scholars claim that the chromatic genus is characterized by a succession of two half tones, and the enharmonic by a succession of two quarter tones, but the Arabs assert that, although this may accidentally happen, it is not at all a necessary feature of these genera. According to al-Fārābī, a chromatic genus is one in which each tetrachord contains a minor third, whatever may be the disposition of the other intervals; an enharmonic genus is one in which each tetrachord contains a major third; and a diatonic genus is one in which each tetrachord contains two full tones.

"Greek authors, in fact, use the denomination *enharmonic*, which Avicenna translates very well by the term *ta'lifiyyah*, to designate the genus that contains the natural third of ratio 5/4, and the denomination *chromatic*, which is exactly translated by the Arab term *mulawwanah*, to designate the genus in which one of the three intervals is a minor third of ratio 6/5 or 7/6."[6]

On the question of quarter tones and their use in the enharmonic genus, the most astonishing theories have been constructed by Western scholars, in which, needless to say, the poor Greeks are always proved to have been wrong. The intemperance of language and imagination shown by scholars can only be attributed to the certainty that the users of equal temperament have lost all notion of the variety of intervals that are harmonically and melodically accurate.

To understand the genera of Greek music, we must first study the fundamental genus, the enharmonic, because in conformity with definitions imported into Greece from Egypt and Asia it was the basic genus of Greek music, from which the others were born. It was by no means a degeneracy or a later refinement of Greek music, as we are sometimes made to believe. Maurice Emmanuel himself had to acknowledge that "it is the enharmonic genus, graphical standard of all the scales, that is the primordial genus,"[7] and he adds, "The professionals stated this strange principle that the most regular, the 'most exact' melodic succession was the enharmonic."[8] Let us see what this genus actually was.

The Enharmonic Genus

According to Western interpretation, the enharmonic genus divides each tetrachord into eight, one, and one *dieses*, that is to say, into a ditone (two major tones) and two quarter tones (ex. 16). This division gives what Maurice Emmanuel calls "ugly little fragments," impossible to sing accurately, if at all:

Example 16.

| Sa | DhaL | Dha1/4 | Pa | Ma | ReL− | Re1/4 | Sa |

> It is difficult to believe that the human voice can commonly permit such an artificial mechanism. The vocal cords, which every singer possesses, do not allow unlimited freedom. A singer is always liable to sing out of tune and to produce unknowingly intervals smaller than the half tone; it is his undeniable right, which he often overuses. But can he at will and with accuracy produce intervals (a third of a tone, a quarter of a tone) without the help of the fundamental consonances (fifth, fourth, natural thirds) to build or measure them accurately?[9]

What the "natural thirds" are, Emmanuel is careful not to say, because there are many different ones and they prove the exact opposite of his thesis. In particular, the third produced by the fundamental consonances of the fifths is the ditone (81/64) and not the natural major third (5/4), which is smaller by one comma. It is the ditone that singers without accompaniment will in many cases sing most easily, and not what is commonly called the natural third (5/4).

The enharmonic genus, says the legend, originated from the pentatonic *vocal enharmonic*, invented by the aulete Olympos (ex. 17). According to Gevaert, the enharmonic was obtained by dividing the half tones to obtain a modal scale of seven tones. This conception somewhat disfigures reality because it brings onto the same level sounds whose function is different.

Example 17.

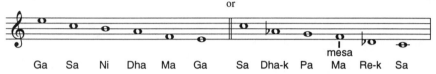

Ga Sa Ni Dha Ma Ga   Sa Dha-k Pa Ma Re-k Sa

In Indian music, the *vocal enharmonic* of Olympos, as it is given here, would correspond to the mode *Gunakalī* (ex. 18). But good musicians, whenever they play or sing a melody in this mode, use two distinct notes for the D♭ (Re komal) as well as for the A♭ (Dha komal). One, generally used in ascending, forms a large half tone with the starting note

Example 18.

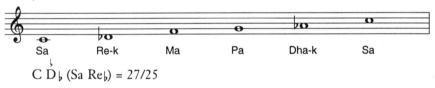

Sa   Re-k   Ma   Pa   Dha-k   Sa

C D♭ (Sa Re♭) = 27/25

in the lower tetrachord, and a major half tone

G A♭ (Pa Dha♭) = 16/15

in the upper one. The large half tone 27/25, which is bigger by one comma than the major half tone, is an unstable interval, but one often used in the ascending scale, to which it gives strength and movement. On the other hand, the A♭ (Dha komal) and D♭ (Re komal) in the descending scale are expressive notes attracted by the fifth and the tonic. Their pitch is therefore necessarily only a minor half tone or a limma above them:

A♭ G (Dha ♯ Pa) = 25/24 and D♭ C (ReL- Sa) = 135/128

This forms an interval full of pathos, which requires resolution to the fifth and the tonic respectively.

There is nothing illogical in this, and all the subtlety of expression of the mode comes from that dash toward joy, which falls back into melancholy. The claim made by Emmanuel and many others that these intervals cannot be clearly differentiated by the ear is unfounded. I have often measured these intervals with very accurate instruments and have always found a perfect accuracy in their differentiation by singers as well as by instrumentalists. In reality, the feeling of these two intervals is so widely different that once they have been heard and understood it is impossible to confuse them. One could have agreed with Emmanuel if he had been satisfied by saying what he knew: that Western singers have become unable to sing accurate intervals because Western vocal as well as instrumental technique always tends to create hazy sounds with strong vibrato, whose purpose is to hide the constant discord of voices and instruments in orchestral music. Unfortunately such a vocal technique diminishes the intensity of expression in equal proportion, and for this reason it is prohibited in Asian music. There is no reason to believe that things were different with the ancient Greeks. When voices and instruments are used without vibrato, the differentiation of intervals becomes clear and musical education quickly permits them to be recognized and reproduced.

The scale of the mode *Gunakalī* can thus be written as in example 19.

Example 19.

| Sa | Re♭ | Ma | Pa | Dha♭ | Sa | Sa | Dha♯ | Pa | Ma | ReL– | Sa |

If we bring together the ascending and descending notes, the scale becomes that shown in example 20.

Example 20.

| Sa | Dha♭ | Dha♯ | Pa | Ma | Re♭ | ReL– | Sa |

The intervals between the notes are:

C	A♭	(Sa Dha♭)	major third	5/4	96 savarts
A	A♭	(Dha Dha♯)	two commas	≈ 46/45	10 savarts
A♭	G	(Dha♯ Pa)	minor half tone	25/24	18 savarts
G	F	(Pa Ma)	major tone	9/8	51 savarts
F	D♭	(Ma Re♭)	small major third	100/81	92 savarts
D♭	D♭	(Re♭ ReL-)	two commas	≈ 46/45	10 savarts
D♭	C	(ReL- Sa)	limma	135/128	23 savarts

When we come to consider Indian scales in detail we shall explain the small difference between the two tetrachords, due to the functional difference between the tonic and the fifth.

In this Indian mode, we thus find an enharmonic division in accordance with Greek and Arabic definitions, which assert that this division is merely the division of the tone into four unequal parts according to harmonic intervals.

This is much more probable and brings us back within the laws of acoustics, from which there is no reason to suppose that Greek music ever went astray. As for the idea of cutting tempered tones into four equal parts, it could only have occurred to the minds of Greek physicists without musical practice or accurate instruments, or to modern Westerners who add to these two handicaps that of being accustomed to the simplified tempered scale, which leads them to forget that several kinds of half tone are used in all the nontempered systems, including Western music. Violinists and singers are usually most surprised if one measures the intervals they are actually using. These often differ widely from those they firmly believe themselves to be reproducing.

Furthermore, it should be remembered that to divide the tone into several intervals does not necessarily mean that one uses intervals smaller than a half tone, because those divisions are never played in succession but only in relation with other notes. In Indian music the interval of one *śruti* is prohibited. Generally one of these so-called quarter tones is used in the ascending scale and the other in the descending scale, as in the case of *Gunakalī*. Even if these two notes are as near as one comma to each other, it does not mean that the comma is used as a musical interval, but simply that the major and minor tone are both used and the difference between these intervals is a comma.

The same mistake appears in the conception that Europeans have of modal music in general. Raouf Yekta Bey remarks that "when speaking of Asian music, people always say that it is composed of small intervals. I do not see any reason for that legend, because the smallest interval used is the limma, whose ratio is 243/256; no interval smaller than the limma is ever used melodically."[10]

No doubt the ancient Greek physicists, already showing a modern spirit, found it amusing to invent numerous ways of dividing the tetrachords. But as their calculations were based on the arithmetical properties of numbers and not on their expressive correspondences, they did not bear the test of experience and were never used in music because they were impractical. Victims today of the same mistake, we cannot understand ancient Greek music because we stop at these amusing calculations instead of looking for the real modes, which necessarily come within the range of acoustically possible intervals.

The enharmonic is not a mode but a genus. The example we gave above shows only one of the numerous modes based on the enharmonic principle that are used by Indian musicians. Many other modes, which apparently belong to other genera, are susceptible to enharmonic interpretation for some of their notes. This interpretation allows an intensification of expression and an increase in the beauty and accuracy of the form. In reality, a careful study will show that in practice every mode has an enharmonic structure. Thus the enharmonic scale is truly, as the Greeks claimed, the fundamental scale of all music and corresponds to the Indian division of the *śrutis*, which is the only rational and indisputable basis of music. If the Greeks maintained a division of twenty-four intervals instead of twenty-two, it was only because they kept (probably for reasons of symmetry) the modifications of the tonic and the fifth, which are never actually used in modal music and are therefore nonexistent. In any event, the accurate division by quarter tones was applicable only to one octave, the other octaves being played by ear and by pulling the strings, as is the case today on the Indian *vīna* and *sitār*. Aristides Quintilianus, in the first century C.E., also said: "The first octave develops in twenty-four *dieses* (quarter tones), and the second rises by half tones."[11] This division is still employed in our day by Turkish and Persian musicians in the tuning of the *tunbur*, and the alleged quarter tones become merely the differences between major and minor tones, major half tones and limmas.

The enharmonic division that we have indicated for the Indian mode *Gunakalī* is not the only possible enharmonic division. In *Gunakalī* the predominant notes (*vādī* and *samvādī*) are first the A♭ (Dha komal), then the D♭ (Re komal), the tonic being C (Sa). From the different data it follows that *Gunakalī* is a morning mode expressing melancholy. If, however, these characteristics change, we can obtain other modes, the scale remaining apparently the same but the tuning of the different notes being adjusted to their new function. The tuning can therefore present slight differences. Without knowing the data that would allow the differentiation of the distinct modes belonging to the enharmonic genus, it is difficult to criticize the measurements given by the Greek physicists, which, though they do not tally, are not necessarily irreconcilable.

Each tetrachord of the enharmonic genus, containing eight, one, and one *dieses*, is divided by different authors as in example 21. If we analyze these ratios

Example 21.

| Sa | Dha-k | Dha-k | Pa | Ma | Re-k | Re-k | Sa |

in the light of the Indian theory of the *śrutis*, we see that 36/35 (12.23 savarts) and 46/45 (9.55 savarts) belong to the same *śruti* and are therefore approximate expressions of the interval of two commas (81/80 x 81/80 = 10.8 savarts). Further, 28/27 (15.8 savarts) and 24/23 (18.48 savarts) belong to the same *śruti*, the minor half tone (25/24 = 17.73 savarts). The scale given by Archytas and that noted here are thus musically, if not arithmetically, identical. Ptolemy's formulation inverts the places of the minor half tone and the double comma. It refers to a different scale, which we also meet in Indian music. The divisions of Didymus and of Boethius form, approximately, tempered quarter tones and are therefore purely theoretical.

Divisions like that of the major half tone into 31/30 x 32/31 = 16/15, or that of the limma into 499/486 x 512/243, are purely conventional and indicate only an approximation to the tempered division represented by comparatively simple ratios, while the tempered division itself is incommensurable. It is therefore useless to attempt to see in them definite intervals or ratios, because their differentiation exists only on paper. This does not mean that if they were actually realized, such differences of intervals could not produce any effect, particularly as a means of action on the inanimate world (in both cases one is an ascending interval and the other a descending one), but such an effect is beyond the range of music proper and can only be produced by the aid of such mechanical means as the Chinese *lü*, for example. As such means do not appear to have been used by the Greeks, these intervals must be considered as approximations. Ignorance of these small artifices of calculation leads to endless classifications of intervals lacking all basis in reality.

The division indicated by the Arabs to find the approximate half of an interval is of this type. The method given by al-Fārābī[12] is as follows: establish the ratio between the numbers representing the two notes forming the interval; multiply each of these numbers by two and, taking half the excess of the greater number over the smaller one, add this half to the smaller and subtract it from the greater. The two ratios obtained divide the interval into approximate halves. For example, to find half of the interval of a fourth (4/3), we shall have:

$$4 \times 2 = 8 \qquad\qquad 3 \times 2 = 6$$
$$8 - 6 = 2 \qquad\qquad 2 : 2 = 1$$
$$6 + 1 = 7 \qquad\qquad 8 - 1 = 7$$

The fourth is thus divided into halves as $8/7 \div 7/6 = 4/3$.

In the same way, the major half tone (16/15) divides into halves as 32/31 x 31/30 = 16/15, the minor tone (10/9) as 20/19 x 19/18 = 10/9, the large tone (8/7) as 16/15 x 15/14 = 8/7, and so forth.

This method has not, so far as we are aware, been explained in those Greek texts still available, although it was obviously used by them. Whenever we meet with a division of this form, we should remember that it stands for an approximation to an equal division, and by no means for two different intervals.

The Chromatic Genus

In the chromatic genus, each tetrachord contains a minor third, and the remaining tone is usually divided into two half tones. This division was, according to the musicians, of six, three, and one *dieses* in each tetrachord, but was simplified by the physicists into six, two, and two *dieses*. To understand these divisions we have to be familiar with the conception of *śrutis* (*dieses*), which can in no way be considered as equal mathematical intervals. An interval of one *śruti* in this case simply means the smallest interval melodically possible above the lowest note of the tetrachord. This interval is generally of one limma (256/243 = 23 savarts) from the tonic, and of a minor half tone (25/24 = 18 savarts) from the fifth. The interval of two *śrutis*, indicated by the physicists for reasons of symmetry, supposing that it were to correspond to a musical reality, could only indicate an interval bigger than the limma by one or two commas, such as the major half tone (16/15 = 28 savarts), for example. It can never represent a double interval, such as the minor tone (two limmas), which is equal to three *śrutis* or *dieses*.

While the enharmonic division of the octave is based on a scale of five notes, the chromatic division normally contains seven notes, and if some of these are subject to the refinements of the enharmonic, these will give a number of additional notes. Just as the enharmonic was taken as the basis for the division into twenty-four *dieses* (or twenty-two *śrutis*), the chromatic will quite naturally be representative of the division of the octave into twelve half tones, and the diatonic will represent the division into seven intervals. But we should be careful not to take literally such classifications, which are more theoretical than practical. There is in reality no discontinuity between the different genera, and almost every mode or scale could be taken as a basis for the establishment of the three fundamental divisions of the octave into twenty-two, twelve, and seven intervals.

Each tetrachord of the chromatic genus is thus divided into a minor third and a tone, as in example 22, the Indian *rāga Dūrgā*. If the tone is divided into two half tones, the scale shown in example 23 results.

Example 22.

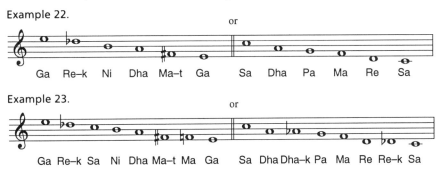

Example 23.

The chromatic genus can be divided into several kinds. The *chromatic of the physicists* or *vulgar chromatic* gives in each tetrachord the intervals 32/27 (trihemitone, 74 savarts), 2187/2048 (apotome, 28 savarts), and 256/243 (limma, 23 savarts). In our notation, this gives the scale shown in example 24.

Example 24.

The two tetrachords are separated by a major tone 9/8.

The *chromatic of the musicians* or *softened chromatic* gives in each tetrachord the intervals 32/27, 243/224, and 28/27. The interval of 248/224 (35.36 savarts) can be identified with the large half tone (27/25 = 33.42 savarts), one comma larger than the major half tone, while that of 28/27 (15.3 savarts) belongs to the same *śruti* as the minor half tone (25/24 = 17.73 savarts). The resulting tuning is shown in example 25.

Example 25.

| Sa | Dha+ | Dha♯ | Pa | Ma | Re | Re♯ | Sa |

In the *vulgar chromatic*, the interval C A+ (Sa Dha+) is a trihemitone (major tone + limma = 32/27). In the *softened chromatic*, C A (Sa Dha) is a minor third (major tone + major half tone = 6/5), one comma larger than in the vulgar chromatic. The interval G A+ (Pa Dha+) is a major tone (9/8) in the *vulgar chromatic* and becomes G A (Pa Dha), a minor tone (10/9), in the *softened chromatic*. This minor tone is divided, according to Didymus, into a major half tone and a minor half tone (16/15 x 25/24 = 10/9), but according to Eratosthenes it is 19/18 x 20/19 = 10/9, which stands for an equal division and is called by the Arabs the *weak chromatic*. According to Ptolemy, the minor tone is divided as 5/14 x 28/27 = 10/9. This produces yet another scale, called by the Arabs the *strong chromatic*.

The *vulgar chromatic* being given as in example 24, the *softened chromatic* will be (1) according to Didymus, 6/5, 25/24, 16/15 (ex. 26);

Example 26.

| Sa | Dha | Dha♭ | Pa | Ma | Re– | ReL+ | Sa |

(2) according to Eratosthenes, 6/5, 19/18, 20/19, the Arabs' *weak chromatic* (ex. 27); and

Example 27.

| Sa | Dha | DhaL | Pa | Ma | Re– | ReL– | Sa |

(3) according to Ptolemy, 6/5, 15/14, 28/27, the Arabs' *strong chromatic* (ex. 28).

Example 28.

| Sa | Dha | Dha♯ | Pa | Ma | Re– | Re♯ | Sa |

We can easily see that in the division of Didymus (minor third, minor half tone, and major half tone), and in that of Ptolemy (minor third, major half tone, and minor half tone), the order of half tones is inverted. The division of Ptolemy is more logical for a descending scale. As for the scale of Eratosthenes, it stands only for a tempered division.

According to the rules of existing modal systems, there can be no mode corresponding to the chromatic scale as it is here represented following the interpretation of Western scholars. But many modes contain the same intervals in a different order, or starting from another note taken as tonic. It is therefore probable that the application of Greek data has been slightly misrepresented.

For example, the Indian *rāga Śrī* is only a plagal form of this scale (ex. 29).

Example 29.

The tonic is C (Sa), but starting from B (Ni) we can easily discover the chromatic tetrachord described by Didymus.

The unification of almost equivalent ratios (such as 28/27 and 25/24, 243/224 and 27/25, 15/14 and 16/15, etc.) on the basis of the Indian theory of the *srutis* may be contested, but this would in no way affect the comparisons we are making. The unification does not affect the relative proportion of the intervals in each mode, and it is easier to deal only with minor or major half tones or their very near approximation than to handle ratios that are difficult to estimate.

The Diatonic Genus

The diatonic genus has the greatest place in the surviving texts on ancient Greek music, because the whole Pythagorean theory of the national harmonies, or Dorian mode, was based on it.

We have already seen that in the diatonic genus each tetrachord was divided into two full tones and one half tone. What those tones and the half tone really were remains somewhat unclear, because the whole modal theory of the Greeks is made obscure by the confusion between the cyclic system of the Pythagoreans, based on the consonance of fifths, and the modal system of the musicians. Unfortunately, it seems that the Greeks themselves felt quite at home in this confusion and never tried to search for its cause. The physicists were so proud of their ideas and so busy imposing them on others that it never occurred to them that both the musicians' system and the enharmonic theory, which the Greeks had also received from Egypt and Asia, were based on a metaphysical system, and that their music illustrated this system and not the Pythagorean, which was always bound to be a poor fit. But the disparity did not disturb the Greek physicists at all. If practice were not in accordance with their theory, it was practice that was wrong, and they went on forcing their theory upon it—

a habit followed also by later Europeans—until nobody could understand anything and the failure was best hidden behind the absurd compromise of temperament. This concession was presented as a great discovery, whereas in reality tempered systems had been known and rejected long before.

But in spite of the efforts of the physicists, musicians went on tuning their instruments, even in the Dorian mode, with the second and the sixth notes one *diesis* lower than the physicists wished them to be; this gives in each tetrachord four, five, and one *dieses*, which according to Archytas are equivalent to the ratios 9/8 (major tone), 8/7 (large major tone), and 28/27 (small minor half tone; see ex. 30).

Example 30.

Ga Re- Sa- Ni Dha Pa- Ma- Ga   Sa NiL+ Dha♯ Pa Ma Ga♯ Re Sa

The physicists, in the meantime, were asking for four, four, and two *dieses*, equivalent to the ratios 9/8 (major tone), 9/8 (major tone), and 256/243 (limma; see ex. 31).

Example 31.

Ga Re- Sa- Ni Dha Pa- Ma- Ga   Sa NiL+ DhaL Pa Ma GaL Re Sa

Thus the great perfect system of the physicists (ex. 32), even in the fundamental Dorian mode, was in reality tuned as in example 33. In other modes the differences were still more striking.

Example 32.

Dha- Pa- Ma- Ga Re- Sa- Ni   Dha Pa- Ma- Ga Re- Sa- Ni (Dha)   Re- Sa- NiL- Dha

Example 33.

Dha- Pa- Ma- Ga Re- Sa- Ni   Dha Pa- Ma- Ga Re- Sa- Ni (Dha)   Re- Sa- Ni♯ Dha

Dorian Harmonies

In Greek music, the general tonic was in the middle of the scale, a fact rather troublesome to modern minds and difficult to understand. But the lowest note was also in many cases taken as tonic, just as the general practice is today. This led to the division of the Dorian mode—which corresponds in the great perfect system (the white keys of the piano or organ) to the octave E to E (Ga to upper Ga)—into two distinct modes.

The first Dorian has for its tonic, fundamental, and final the lowest note, E (Ga), as in example 34. It corresponds to what the Indians call *Sa grāma*, having the Madhyamā (*mesa*), the modern tonic, as its fourth note. If we transpose it into the Hypodorian tone (*mesa* F[Ma]), whose tonic is C (Sa), the first Dorian is written like the Indian scale *Shat*, as in example 35.

Example 34.

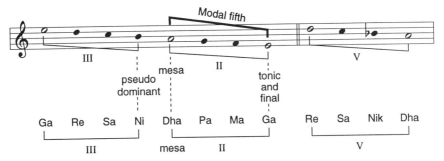

Example 35.

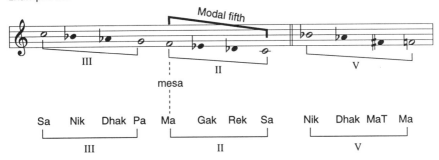

In the second Dorian mode, the *mesa* is both the fundamental and the tonic (ex. 36). This corresponds to what Indian treatises call *Ma grāma*, that is, a scale in which the *mesa* (Madhyamā) is tonic and fundamental.

Example 36.

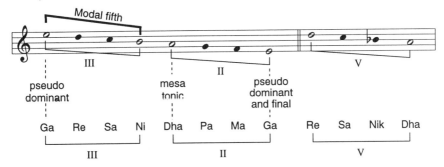

If, considering the *mesa* as true tonic, we start the scale from it, and then transpose the second Dorian into the Phrygian tone (*mesa* C [Sa]), we obtain the familiar Indian scale *Yavanpūrī Tōḍī* (Aeolian mode). By adding the conjunct tetrachord (V) this scale is changed into that of *Bhairavī* (ex. 37).

Example 37.

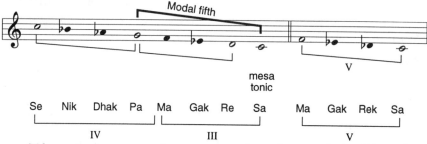

Take again the great perfect system, as shown in example 38. We see here that on the fixed degrees (the "body of harmony") we can establish two other modes, the Aeolian and the Mixolydian, which, with the two Dorians, complete the group of Dorian harmonies.

Example 38.

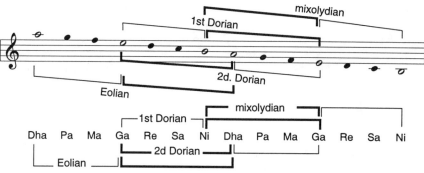

Corresponding to the octave A to A (Dha to upper Dha), the Aeolian mode has the same modal fifth as the second Dorian, but develops into the highest tetrachord (ex. 39).

Example 39.

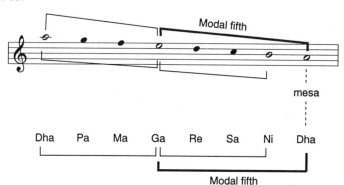

Transposed into the Phrygian tone, the Aeolian mode appears as *Yavanpūrī Toḍī* (ex. 40).

Example 40.

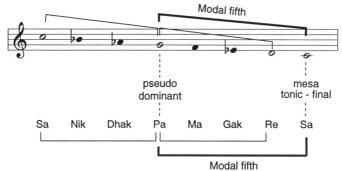

Corresponding to the octave B to B (Ni to upper Ni), the Mixolydian has the same modal fifth as the first Dorian, but develops into the lowest tetrachord. Its modal fifth is therefore in the upper part of the octave, and this classifies it as belonging to the *Ma grāma* (tonic on the fourth; ex. 41).

Example 41.

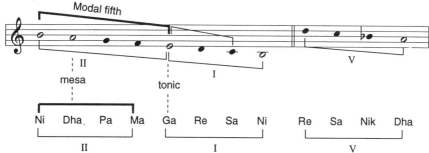

Transposed into the Hypodorian tone, the Mixolydian appears as in example 42.

Example 42.

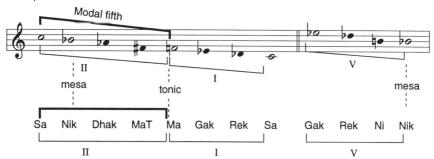

Exotic Harmonies

The harmonies of the exotic Phrygio-Lydian group had as their base the mobile sounds of the great perfect system.

The Phrygian mode was formed by the octave D to D (Re to upper Re). Having its modal fifth in the upper part of the octave, it comes within the category of *Ma grāma*. It had the same modal scale as the Ionian or Iasti, also called Hypophrygian, but the latter, belonging to the *Sa grāma*, developed upward. The fundamental of these two modes was the G (Pa; ex. 43).

Example 43.

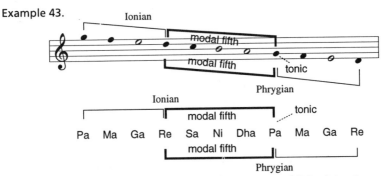

The Lydian and Hypolydian modes were established in the same way, around the modal fifth, whose fundamental is F (Ma). The former belongs to the category of the *Ma grāma*, the latter to that of the *Sa grāma* (ex. 44).

Example 44.

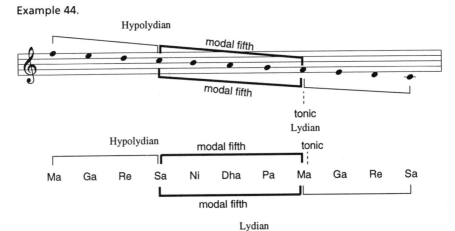

The Greeks considered the *Ma grāma* (tonic on the fourth) to be the basic system. They expressed the relation of the *Sa* to the *Ma* grâma by the prefix *hypo*, which indicates the relation of two modes having the same modal fifth but complementing the octave either downward (normal mode) or upward (subsidiary mode = *hypo*). This conception may be the origin of the classification of authentic and plagal modes in Gregorian music. Thus the Ionian mode was also called Hypophrygian and the Aeolian mode Hypodorian. Only the first Dorian, probably because of its national character, remained free from this nominal servitude in regard to the Mixolydian, which also kept its ancient name.

Transposed into the Hypodorian tone, the Ionian mode becomes the scale shown in example 45. Without the conjunct tetrachord this would be the scale of *Chāyānatta*, and with the conjunct tetrachord, that of *Jaijavantī*.

Example 45.

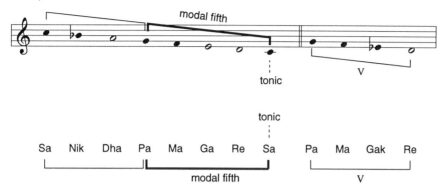

The Phrygian mode can be expressed by the same scale continued downward, or by the scale shown in example 46. Without the conjunct tetrachord it resembles the scale of the Indian mode *Kāfī*.

Example 46.

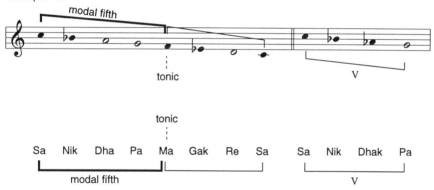

Similarly the Hypolydian mode, transposed into the Hypodorian tone, (tonic C [Sa]) becomes the scale shown in example 47. Without the conjunct tetrachord it is the scale of the Indian mode *Yāman;* with the conjunct it is *Gaur-Sārang.*

Example 47.

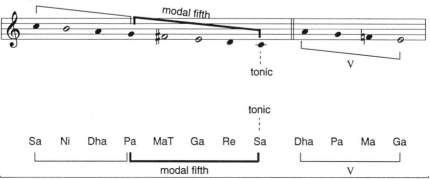

The Lydian mode remains as shown in example 48. Without the conjunct tetrachord it resembles the scale of *Nata*, and with the conjunct tetrachord, that of *Khammaj*.

Example 48.

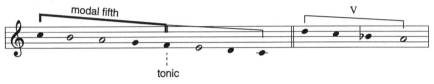

In the great perfect system, the notes C and D (Sa and Re) are never used as fundamental. The only scales starting from C (Sa) and D (Re) are those of the Phrygian and Lydian, which both have their tonic on their fourth note, respectively F (Ma) and G (Pa).

It is very interesting to note that those essential modes of modern music, the major mode of C (Sa) and the minor mode of D (Re), were considered as unpleasant and were forbidden by the Greeks and probably all peoples of ancient times, and although they were classified by the Indians, they were not given any prominence by them until recent times. Maurice Emmanuel remarks, "The modes of D [Re] and C [Sa] had been banished from the Greek musical language. . . . There was among the Greeks and their successors, the primitive *cantores* of the Christian Church, a sort of repulsion for the modes D A D [Re Dha Re] and C G C [Sa Pa Sa]. We shall note that our major mode is among the two proscribed ones; it was later to take its revenge. As for the modern pseudo-minor . . . it emerged from the D A D [Re Dha Re] scale."[13]

We can find here a remarkable confirmation of the theory which states that, since the fundamental modes are connected with the cosmic developments of the cycle, only those modes that are related to the cosmic condition of a certain period appear natural during that period. In India as in Europe the ancient Dorian mode (*Bhairavī*), the mode of E (Ga), has slowly given way to the mode of D (Re), *Kāfī*, as basic scale, only to be replaced in turn by the mode of C (Sa) *Bilāval*.

When we study the significance of the notes according to Indian theory in greater detail, we come to understand why the major mode was formerly rejected. We see that its intervals express materialism, sensual egotism, hardness, and other qualities that could not be given a dominant place in art so long as it was subordinate to considerations of an intellectual and spiritual order.

When we want to pass from the abstract theory of the great perfect system to musical practice, we immediately notice the discrepancy. All these modes were in use before their classification was made, and this way of bringing different modes within the frame of one scale, however clever it may be, does not, nor can it ever, fully correspond to the reality of modal systems. Therefore, the tuning of the notes in the general scale corresponds only approximately to the actual tuning for each mode. The tuning of all the notes in a mode is done in relation to the tonic of that mode, and one may not arbitrarily choose any note as fundamental. If this is done, the modes so obtained can only be pseudo-modes, plagal forms of the original scale, though they may outwardly appear to be independent modes.

For any of these pseudo-modes to become a real mode, the tuning of each note would have to be adjusted so as to establish, with the new tonic, the ratios that would justify this function. At first sight the notes might appear the same, but in reality they present differences of one or two commas. This changes their expression and allows for the establishment of logical ratios.

We shall meet with similar adjustments of tuning in Western music every time we pass from the cyclic system, upon which all modulations and transposition depend, to the modal system, which rules chords and modes, since it is the modal system that allows the establishment of harmonic ratios in relation to a basic sound. Disregard of these differences leads inevitably to the dead end of temperament, as Aristoxenes had foreseen, because in tempered systems, both chord and modulation are equally wrong, and at least neither can be said to have been sacrificed to the other.

The classification of modes, as well as the interesting divisions used by Greek physicists, seem bound to remain mere abstractions and amusing mental gymnastics as presented by western scholars. These divisions do not correspond to any acoustic or metaphysical system, but rather seem a play upon the arithmetical properties of numbers—a game to which modern scientists are also prone. It by no means follows that ancient Greek music was not as marvelous as has been described; the calculations of physicists are simply not the place to look for such marvels.

All the intervals used in musical practice are necessarily based upon those simple acoustic intervals that can be sung easily, can be recognized by the ear, and represent definite and distinct expressions—expressions that can be determined with the help of the Indian division of the *śrutis*. Therefore when the Arab Hellenists assert that the intervals used by the Greeks were the minor tone, the limma, and the apotome, which together divide the major tone into four unequal intervals, it is highly probable that they are right.

The Fifteen Tones of Transposition

In Greek music it is important not to mistake modal scales (*mūrchanas*) for tones (pitches of tonic), as Boethius himself so awkwardly did.

The tones are only a system of transposition, similar to the modern Western system, by which any mode can be brought to a pitch easily practicable for singers or instruments. They are classified according to the respective pitches of the *mesa*. The fundamental tone being the Hypolydian, whose *mesa* is the A (Dha) of the Greek unaltered scale, its exact pitch would be, in the modern Western standard of pitch, F ♯ (*Ma tīvra*), approximately the Ga of the usual Indian pitch.

Here is the list of the different tones:

Tone	*Mesa*
Hyperlydian	upper G (Pa)
Hyperaeolian	upper F♯ (Ma tīvra)
Hyperphrygian	upper F (Ma)
Hyperiastian	upper E (Ga)
Hyperdorian	upper E♭ (Ga komal)
Lydian	upper D (Re)
Aeolian	upper D♭ (Re komal)
Phrygian	upper C (Sa)
Iastian	middle B (Ni)
Dorian	middle B♭ (Ni komal)
Hypolydian	middle A (Dha)
Hypoaeolian	middle A♭ (Dha komal)
Hypophrygian	middle G (Pa)
Hypoiastian	middle F♯ (Ma tivra)
Hypodorian	middle F (Ma)

Chapter Seven

THE WESTERN SCALE
AND EQUAL TEMPERAMENT

UT*queant laxis*   REsonare fibris
MIra gestorum   FAmuli tuorum
SOLve polluti   LAbii reatum
            Sancte Iohannes
                    Hymn to Saint John the Baptist

Western Music

The Western musical system has emerged from a mixture of various traditions that, because of complete confusion in the theoretical definitions, were brought together in a rather haphazard way. The resulting system is cyclic, with constant changes of tonic (modulations), but on each tonic, and on each note of the scales based on these tonics, the establishment of chords (harmony) depends upon the modal system, since the different notes of a chord take their meaning from their relation to the fundamental note of the chord. This system would have had every advantage had it not been based upon a fundamental confusion: the notes that form consonant chords are not the same as the notes required for modulation.[1]

As long as music was kept within certain limits of simplicity, musicians could, even in an orchestra, adjust each note to the successive necessities of harmony and modulation by instinct. But such adaptations, if they are not accurately done, render the expression hazy and confused, and this imprecision compelled composers to complicate the structure of chords in an attempt to render their meaning more definite. But these complications finally resulted only in more confusion. It would have been sufficient to play the simpler chords accurately for their meaning to become clear and attractive. Added to this, the generalized use of equal temperament, which vastly oversimplifies musical structures, has led people to forget completely the most elementary acoustic realities and, by distorting all the intervals, has rendered the meaning of chords vague and unclear. It is generally said that the ear can recognize the true interval represented by the tempered interval. This is a fact; but each ear makes a different adaptation according to individual tendencies, and the same chord may have a different significance for different people according to their mood. The meaning of an accurate chord, on the other hand, is determined absolutely and perceived by all.

The result is that Westerners have more and more lost all conception of a music able to express clearly the highest ideas and feelings. They now expect from music mostly a confused noise, more or less agreeable, but able to arouse in the audience only the most ordinary sensations and simplified images. This is a complete misconception of the true role of music. As Plato said, "Music, whose movements are of the same kind as the regular revolutions of our soul, does not appear, to the man who has intelligent intercourse with the Muses, to be good merely for giving physical pleasure, as seems to be the case in our day. On the contrary, the Muses have given us music as an ally of our soul in its attempt to bring back order and harmony into those periodic movements that had become disorderly in us."[2] But who in modern times tries to have intelligent intercourse with the Muses? People strive only for technical progress that allows virtuosity, and for extravagant theories that make their authors famous!

> Zarlino, to whom we owe the theoretical principles on which our modern theory rests . . . though he well knew the legitimate proportions that should be those of diatonic, chromatic, and enharmonic tones, and although he recognized that it is these proportions that are given by nature and science, by Pythagoras and Plato, nevertheless created a series of artificial and wrong intonations following Ptolemy, to conform himself, he said, to the march of counterpoint, which makes them necessary. Thus, according to him, *harmony is only made possible by the violation of the principles of harmony*, and one cannot form chords without making voices and instruments discordant. . . . Salinas . . . who otherwise fights Zarlino . . . agrees with him on this point and sincerely believes, like him, that one must abandon the accuracy of sounds in order to build a simultaneous harmony. . . . The Italian authors . . . adopted the artificial proportions of this theorist although they all recognized them to be wrong. The famous Rameau in France and Martini in Italy had only one aim . . . that is, to find a basis for those proportions which they believed to be necessary for harmony.[3]

It is often proudly asserted that the modern Western musical system is sufficient to express everything, but the slightest true contact with other musical systems immediately proves the opposite. The power of evocation of the harmonic system as it is conceived today is weak and confused if compared with any modal system. It oscillates between abstractions and extremely conventional imitative harmonies, because what is called an imitation of a bird, the wind, the rain, a fountain, a factory, or any other much-used subject is in reality so far from the model that a deep knowledge of musical conventions is required to be able to see the connection. Such conventions can become so familiar that one believes them to be realities and derives from them real pleasure, but anyone unfamiliar with them could never guess what it is all about. The idea of representing natural phenomena, or the movements of things and beings, by imitating the noises they make appears childish to the Eastern way of thinking; it is really a primitive conception, in the sense nowadays given to this word. The relations of sounds should be able to express, not the noise or the external appearance of things, but their essence. The knowledge of these subtle relations has always been considered the basis and the true object of art in the East. It is because of these relations that the effect of music can be so deep and directly perceptible without requiring any conventions or taxing the imagination of hearers. For example, when the Indian mode of the rains, *Megh-Mallar*, is played, no sound will attempt to imitate the noise of raindrops or of thunder, but the relations between the sounds will be so similar to those between the elements when a storm is approaching that not only trained musicians but even animals will inevitably feel the rain in the air.

Modern Western music was able to develop its polyphonic system only by deliberately sacrificing the greater part of its possibilities and breaking the ties that connected it with other musical systems. Formerly, all musical systems were close to each other and, in spite of differences, could generally be understood from one country to another. Hence the success that the musicians who came with the Turkish empress had in China, or that some African musicians had in the Muslim world during the first centuries of Islam, or that gypsies have had in Europe. But since the Middle Ages there has been a tendency in the West to accept those simplifications of the theory that had already been rejected everywhere else as being incompatible with a refined form of art. Therefore, when Guido d'Arezzo (990–1040), "having reduced everything to the diatonic and given the last blow to the quarter tones inherited from Greek melody, directs our scale toward temperament and facilitates the progress of polyphony," he really only gives a blow to folk music, whose very complex modal and rhythmic forms will give way to a heavy and simplified official art.

Fabre d'Olivet explains that voices are

> compelled by certain instruments—particularly those used in musical education such as the piano, the harpsichord, the harp, or the guitar—to follow artificial intonations, and in turn compel all the other instruments that accompany them to take those intervals in the same way, so as not to be out of tune. Consequently, our diatonic genus is sometimes correct and sometimes incorrect, our chromatic is always incorrect, and we have no enharmonic genus. We must admit that if, as has been suggested by Zarlino, Salinas, and Martini, and as Rameau believed, we adopted such a system in order to have some sort of harmony, our harmony surely does not deserve the name, and it would have been better to keep it Gothic name

of counterpoint; we must also realize that our symphonists have no reason to be astonished if their modern music does not produce the effects of ancient music, since they do not hesitate to infringe the true laws of nature in this way and to corrupt the sensitivity of the ear to the point of habituating this organ to receive three wrong sounds out of the diatonic seven, never to hear a correct chromatic sound, and to be completely ignorant of the charms of the enharmonic genus. Had the Greeks had a musical system similar to ours, I would find it difficult to believe in the marvels of which they were proud, because I should see a definite contradiction between the weakness of the cause and the strength of the effect.[5]

Following such deformations, the Western musical language finds itself artificially aloof from acoustic realities and from the laws on which the metaphysical correspondences of sounds are based, a fact that renders it incomprehensible to other people. Therefore when circumstances compel peoples like the Malayans or African Americans to adopt the Western musical system, they quickly transform it back into logical modal forms. This is why their songs, though usually very simple, have such an emotional appeal.

The Modes of Plainchant

Very little is known today about the modal forms used in Europe during the Middle Ages. There remain very few documents and no means of comparison with existing modal systems. In the Middle Ages, musical systems were not isolated from each other as they later became. It seems for example that in Spain, when Alfonso the Wise introduced the teaching of music into the University of Salamanca, there were numerous points of comparison between Christian art as codified by Saint Ambrose and Saint Gregory, ancient art as explained by Boethius, and Arab art as defined by Avicenna in conformity with Greek tradition. The reforms of Guido d'Arezzo had not yet ruined either popular art or the rich musical heritage that the troubadours were spreading from one end of Europe to the other. In our times it is mostly in the Nordic countries that some remnant of this "preharmonic" art of the West has survived, and the transcriptions attempted by Grieg, imperfect as they are, can give us at least an idea of this powerful and vigorous art now almost lost.

The only trace of medieval music that has kept some vitality in the West is the religious music called plainchant, codified by Saint Gregory. Although extremely simplified, it has to this day kept a system similar to that of the Greek *Doristi* (the Dorian modes and their plagal forms). The main difference is that the medieval modes develop upward instead of downward and that the fundamental of the first tone is the seventh of the Dorian mode, the D (Re). The conjunct tetrachord, which contains an augmented fourth, became an integral part of some of these modes, and so we may often get an idea of what the practice of Greek modes was more easily from the simplified Gregorian modes than from the theory of the *Doristi*, which was made too abstract by a desire for symmetry.

The eight modes of plainchant were imported from the East by Gregory the Great (540–604 C.E.), who, on return from his post of ambassador in Constantinople, codified them in his famous *Antiphonary*. They are a transcription of Byzantine modes similar to the eight modes that the patriarch Severus of Antioch had used for tropes in the fourth century. Unfortunately, during their journey to Rome these modes had lost the essential element of their differentiation; namely, the measuring element, the pedal of the tonic, the Byzantine *ison*, the essential element of all modal music that defines each tone and the expression of each note. These melodies are thus devoid of a basis and have a rather peculiar lack of definition and absence of expression. Furthermore, their classification is as arbitrary as it is incomplete, because it has as its principle the permutation of the tonic, inspired by the Greek *Doristi*, a system that is based on the peculiar concordance of certain modes; it can be used as a means of classification but can in no way be taken as the basis of modal structure. This is why the modes of plainchant do not represent the system of metaphysical correspondences that Saint Gregory thought he had discovered. Gregory had not at all understood the basis of the system he pretended to adopt. He was a violent enemy of pre-Christian culture and whenever he could get hold of ancient books he had them burned. This was obviously not the best way to understand them! The modifications he brought to the modes and the substitution of hexachords for tetrachords are not justifiable and serve no purpose.

Although they are deprived of their true expression because of these deformations and the lack of certain elements, the Gregorian modes are nevertheless by their structure real modes and therefore keep a certain appearance that rules their use. Formerly this use was strictly regulated and the mixture of modes was considered a sin. This is why, "in spite of the permission given by King Louis IX to form an academy of music, the Parliament of Paris had it closed on the grounds that musicians did not observe the ecclesiastical rules and were passing too frequently from one mode or genus to another."[6] At the time of the Reformation, Luther was still keeping to custom and saying that the Gospel should be set to the sixth tone because Christ is a gentle Lord whose words are lovely, whereas, Saint Paul being a grave Apostle, the Epistle should be set to the eighth tone.

Unlike the Greek modes, the Gregorian modes are still in use, so it is easy to verify their definitions and compare them with Indian *rāgas*, as shown in example 49. Where the definitions of Greek modes seem sufficiently clear, the same example indicates their correspondences with the modes of plainchant, disregarding the erroneous medieval correspondences due to Boethius's confusion of modes and tones. Four of the Gregorian modes are authentic; four are plagal. In example 49 the final of each mode is marked with an F, and the dominant (*vādī*) with a D.

Example 49. The Eight Gregorian Modes

First mode (authentic): *uddha a¯ja mūrchhana* (Phrygian)

Re Ga Ma Pa Dha Nik Ni Sa Re   Sa Re Gak Ma Pa Dhak Dha Nik Sa

Second mode (plagal): *Yavanpurī Todī*

Dha Ni Sa Re Ga Ma Pa Dha   Sa Re Gak Ma Pa Dhak Nik Sa

Third mode (authentic): *Bhairavī* (first Dorian)

Ga Ma Pa Dha Ni Sa Re Ga   Sa Rek Gak Ma Pa Dhak Nik Sa

Fourth mode (plagal): *A'v'kr'nta mūrchhana* (first Dorian)

Ni Sa Re Ga Ma Pa Dha Nik Ni   Sa Rek Gak Ma MaT Dhak Nik Ni Sa

Fifth mode (authentic): *Gaur-Sārang* (Hypolydian)

Ma Pa Dha Nik Ni Sa Re Ga Ma   Sa Re Ga Ma MaT Pa Dha Ni Sa

Sixth mode (plagal): *Khammaj*

Sa Re Ga Ma Pa Dha Nik Ni Sa

Seventh mode (authentic): *Matsar'k°ta mūrchhana*

Eighth mode (plagal): *Kāfī* (Phrygian)

The first and the eighth modes are forms of the Phrygian mode, the third and the fourth are forms of the first Dorian, the fifth mode is a form of the Hypolydian, and the sixth and seventh modes belong to the Hypophrygian-Ionian-Hypolydian group.

The Scale of Zarlino

After numerous changes, mostly due to the attempts of theorists to adapt an incomplete and poorly understood Greek theory to an altogether different musical practice, the scale that was to be the basis of Western modern music was finally established by the Italian theorist Gioseffo Zarlino (1540–94) on the ruins of popular music.

"What are the elements of our modern system, according to the generally accepted theory of Zarlino?" asks Fabre d'Olivet. And he answers:

> Of seven diatonic sounds, C, D, E, F, G, A, B, [Sa, Re, Ga, Ma, Pa, Dha, Ni], three, C [Sa], F [Ma], and G [Pa], are correct; one, D [Re], is correct or incorrect according to whether it is considered as the *fifth* of G [Pa] or as the *sixth* of F [Ma]; and three, E [Ga], A [Dha], and B [Ni], are completely wrong. These seven diatonic sounds give fourteen chromatic sounds, since they can all be altered into sharps [*tīvra*] and flats [*komal*]. But these fourteen chromatic sounds are all, without exception, wrong. As for the enharmonic sounds, they simply do not exist.[7]

Zarlino takes the first five notes of the scale of fifths and reduces them to the nearest equivalent notes in the series of relations to the tonic:

Series of fifths		Zarlino's notes	
C (Sa)	1	C (Sa)	1
D (Re)	9/8	D (Re)	9/8

Series of fifths		Zarlino's notes (continued)	
E+ (Ga+)	81/64	E (Ga)	5/4
G (Pa)	3/2	G (Pa)	3/2
A+ (Dha+)	27/16	A (Dha)	5/3
		C (Sa)	2

To these are added the two accessory degrees:

a fifth down from C (Sa)	F (Ma)	4/3
a fourth down from E (Ga)	B (Ni)	15/8

In the very elaboration of this scale, we are already changing from an ascending cyclic structure to a descending modal one. This gives us the scale known by the name of Zarlino:

	C	D	E	F	G	A	B	C
	(Sa)	(Re)	(Ga)	(Ma)	(Pa)	(Dha)	(Ni)	(Sa)
ratios:	1	9/8	5/4	4/3	3/2	5/3	15/8	2
intervals:		9/8	10/9	16/15	9/8	10/9	9/8	16/15
savarts:		51	46	28	51	46	51	28

The intervals are of three different types: major tone 9/8, minor tone 10/9, and major half tone 16/15. Therefore, when the tonic is changed, we shall obtain sharps and flats of different natures, and the very notes of the original scale will in some cases have to be raised or lowered by one comma (the difference between the major and minor tone). This difficulty comes from the fact that certain notes of the scale of fifths, which alone allows transposition, have been replaced by the ratios that allow correct harmonic intervals. In reality, for modulation, one is compelled to come back to the scale of fifths. In practice, therefore, two scales are used conjointly in Western music, and not, as is generally believed, only the Zarlino scale. This ambiguous position, never fully clarified, has led to the general adoption of temperament, which by splitting the difficulty between the various intervals apparently suppresses the problem but does not solve it.

In order to obtain exactly the same scale when modulating from one major key to the neighboring major key, the fourth of the first key has to be raised by one limma and the sixth by one comma, the new tonic being the fifth of the former key. Thus from the very first modulation we obtain two notes that do not belong to the scale of Zarlino. In the sharp keys all the notes are raised in this way, one after the other, by one comma; for each additional sharp, another note is so raised. Conversely, if the modulation moves downward by fifths, notes are successively lowered by one comma.

The keys with sharps have their original notes raised one after the other by a comma (to which a sharp is later added), while the keys with flats have their original notes lowered one after the other by a comma (to which a flat is later added). The result can be that the flats are lower than the corresponding sharps, as musicians often notice, despite the objection of the physicists that the reverse should be true since the sum of the theoretical intervals represented by the sharp and the flat is less than one tone. This is simply because the natural notes (*śuddha*) to which these sharps and flats have been added are no longer the notes of the original C (Sa) scale, but notes that are lower in the case of the flat and higher in the case of the sharp. For example, when we modulate from C major into G major, the A is raised by one comma to become A+. When we later modulate into B major (which is really B+ major), the sharp will be added to the A+, giving A♯ L+. Likewise, the B♭ of B♭ minor, being itself B♭ L+, happens to be the same note as the A♯ of B+ major. But the B♭ L- of D♭ major is one comma lower, or B♭ , and is therefore lower than the A♯ of A+ major.

We can see from this example that all the respective positions of sharps and flats are possible and that to say in a general way that sharps are higher than flats or the reverse is completely meaningless. The problem is really not very complicated, and it would be better to consider it as it is rather than to discuss it endlessly on insufficient data. Besides, we are speaking here only of the flats and sharps necessary to obtain the same scale again after modulation. In addition to these there are other flats and sharps necessary for expression, which are used by good musicians and are different again. From this it is easy to understand how inadequate is the scale of Zarlino.

If we follow the progression of scales with sharps and the progression of scales with flats, the keys of apparently similar tonics (F♯ and G♭ , or B♮ and C♭, for example) can never coincide because their tonics are different from one another by one or two commas. It is therefore always incorrect to pass from one to the other, or rather, if this be done it produces relations of a new kind, which it would be necessary to define if their effect were to be correctly used. However, a sharp and a flat may in some instances happen to coincide.

Being based on the cycle of fifths, the chain of modulations can never come back to its original pitch. It can, like the cycle of fifths itself, by symbolized by an infinite spiral.

The Major Mode

It was only in Basel in 1547 that Glareanus, in his *Dodecachordon*, introduced the major mode, which he calls the Ionian mode, as the fundamental scale. In India, the major mode was to be accepted as a basic scale, under the name of *rāga Bilāval*, only in 1813 in the *Nagmat e asaphi* of Muhammad Rezza.

Among the combinations of successive or simultaneous sounds that have simple ratios between them, the major mode is only one particular case. Its melodic characteristics are not particularly expressive, but it allows the formation of chords on its various degrees that by their structure are somewhat similar to the harmonics of a single sound. It therefore allows transposition from one degree to another with only a small adjustment of tuning, and in order to hide its monotony, Western musicians constantly use these changes of tonic, which to the Easterner appear artificial, of little significance, and therefore scarcely justified.

In order to achieve those perfect chords that a refined ear perceives in the single yet complex sound of a well-tuned instrument, Westerners have sacrificed all the possibilities of modes, which are as different from each other in their structure and possibilities as a square from a circle, a triangle, or a star-shaped polygon. Modes open unlimited possibilities of chords, which we can sometimes catch glimpses of through the temperament, because temperament, by disfiguring the major mode, has brought it onto an equal footing with many other modes equally disfigured by it. This explains why so many harmonic "discoveries" followed the widespread use of the modern piano. Until then, the major mode ruled because, as Maurice Emmanuel explained, the Western minor mode is only a variation of the major mode, that tyrant of Western music.

In addition to the peculiarity of harmonic transposition, the major mode is, by its structure, no more natural than many others, and even less pleasant for the ear than modes presenting a more complete series of harmonics. We prefer it mostly out of habit, and we see when we study the symbolism and the emotional correspondences of notes according to Indian theory that the intervals of the major mode are those that indicate egotism, vanity, materialism, and the search for pleasure, thus forming a frame in which the mentality of our times finds itself completely at home. But Westerners, who appear to ignore the fact that all the elements of their music were originally borrowed from Egypt and Chaldea, have no idea of the significance of the notes they use, and they wonder at their own genius when they discover that some chords can express precise emotions, whereas these same expressions have been defined for thousands of years in those very *śāstras* which gave the first definitions of these intervals and chords.

Let us now see how one Western musicologist explains the major mode. Ernest Britt writes:

> It is in vain that the explanation of the modern scale has been sought in the physical phenomenon of the vibration of sonorous bodies. . . . This disposition of elements presents itself, in our diatonic scale, in a concrete and rigorously logical form, otherwise it could never have produced either its own synthesis, or the symphony, or the musical drama, or any of the harmonic forms that are the originality of modern music. And if the rationalism of the Western genius has been able to triumph over traditional mistakes, if it has been able to create a melodic and harmonic organ so complete and so perfectly adapted to the expression of human feelings, it

is no doubt because the constitution of the modern scale corresponds to some law of inner organization of psychic essence, whose imperious necessity could only be felt at the time when the mental development of humanity was sufficiently advanced to receive its revelation and conceive of its reality.[8]

One could not find expressed in a more blatant form the perverted reasoning that deprives so many otherwise well-documented works of Westerners of all serious scientific value, and we wonder whether Britt would really be ready to defend the logical implications of his words. He would apparently have us believe that harmonic forms exist only in modern music, that modern Western music alone is capable of expressing human feelings, that others than Westerners are consequently either not humans or are deprived of feelings, or, if they have feelings, have no means of expressing them, that Aristotle and Śaṅkarāchārya were mentally deficient since human beings had not attained mental development before modern times, that the secrets of harmony have been "revealed" to some modern Moses by a benevolent Jehovah delighted at the good behavior of our contemporaries, and so on.

In general the reasoning of Western scholars in relation to music could be summarized as follows: The Western scale is not correct according to the laws of physics or mathematics, but, being used by Westerners, it is superior to all others. Since it is in contradiction with physical laws, it must therefore be the expression of some superior psychic law, still unknown to us, but which is the measure of genius and progress. That such methods of reasoning could be printed and accepted certainly does not indicate that the mental development of humanity has yet attained the elements of logic, and if nobody objects to it, it is probably because the superiority of everything European is an article of faith that should not be discussed.

I hope I will be excused for criticizing so harshly these unfortunate remarks of Ernest Britt, whose works are otherwise well documented and show a real spirit of research. I do so only in the hope that we may understand how high is the wall of prejudice behind which so many Westerners are imprisoned, a prejudice that makes their reasoning absurd and out of place whenever a question relating to other civilizations is involved. Unfortunately, their mistake is difficult to cure because they are not even conscious of being unfair, since they know nothing of the logical methods of discussion taught, for example, by the Indians, of which the Greeks had some idea, and which allow the criticism of arguments and the establishment of logical relations between cause and effect.

Equal Temperament

When a musical scale is established starting from a fundamental sound, that scale easily remains within the limits of harmonic sounds and simple proportions. But when, starting from another note of that scale, we try to constitute a scale or chords similar to the first one, some of the notes obtained do not coincide with those of the first scale. In order to simplify the musical problem and the construction of fixed-scale instruments, Western musicians neglect these differences and, choosing an intermediate sound, declare that the ear adapts itself to it and does not perceive the difference. All modes and chords are thus reduced to a series of twelve sounds, among which none has a correct relation to the others. But this system is not really sufficient for melody or successive harmony, nor for simultaneous harmony. Small differences of pitch may, in the case of an isolated note, appear negligible to an untrained ear. But when notes are brought together in a mode, these slight differences of pitch will bring about considerable differences in the expressive significance of the mode. Similarly, when the notes are grouped in the shape of chords, these same small differences of pitch will create beats (variations of intensity) between the sounds, which besides being unpleasant greatly diminish the significance of the chords.

We cannot see exactly if one brick is slightly bigger than another, yet when we come to build we see immediately a great difference between a straight and regular wall and one where nothing is level; in the same way, even if we cannot perceive the difference between individual notes, the difference is extremely apparent between a pure chord and a chord that beats—and in the tempered scale every chord beats.

If we carefully examine the structure of the modern Western musical system, however vague its theory may be as described in treatises on harmony, it is not impossible to find in it the elements of a logical and coherent system. But this system is very different from the artificial tempered scale actually in use, which, while it gives some facilities of execution, has twisted the development of modern musical thought in a strange direction. The tempered scale to a considerable extent hides from us the thoughts of the great masters of the past, whose most deep and noble works can appear monotonous and childish when they are so disfigured. But this is difficult to realize, because modern people have so lost their sensitivity to simple chords and modal degrees considered in relation to a tonic that they can never believe that a single note can perfectly well create an effect that not even a massive chord can produce upon their calloused minds.

Helmholtz has said, "The music based on the tempered scale must be considered as an imperfect music. . . . If we suppose it or even find it beautiful, it means that our ear has been systematically spoiled since childhood."[9] In the words of A. Langel, "The ear became accustomed to the continual approximations of temperament only at the cost of a part of its natural sensitivity."[10]

Equal temperament is in no way a new thing. It has been invented many times by those half scholars who always come in to explain and improve that which they do not fully understand. In China, for example, "He Chengtian

[370–447 C.E.] and Lü Zhuo [d. 610 C.E.] opposed the system of Jing Fang, that is, the indefinite progression of perfect fifths. They wanted to force the numbers corresponding to the *lin zhong* [G (Pa)], and to all the *lü*, so that the *zhong lü* [F+ (Ma+), the eleventh fifth] would again give birth to the *huang zhong* [C (Sa)], and the complete cycle be limited to twelve *lü*."[11]

We must again repeat that it is not possible to create music with sounds that have no relation between themselves, and that the simpler the ratios between sounds are, the more their relation is harmonious, while the more complicated the ratios are, the more dissonant are the sounds. This is why equal temperament is musically absurd, because it replaces the simple ratios of the notes (4/3, 5/4, 9/8, 10/9, etc.) with ratios that are near to them but are nevertheless extremely complicated. The ratio of the tempered half tone is something like 1,059,463,094/1,000,000,000, while the major half tone is 16/15 and the minor half tone 25/24. The tempered intervals are therefore exceedingly dissonant and create in every chord such beats that only people whose ears are hardened by the habit of noise, or musicians who follow the musical thought so intensely that they do not hear the false notes of the instruments, can bear them.

Equal temperament has had a strange effect on some of the musicians of the present generation. As they have never heard a consonant chord, they know the chords only as more or less acute dissonances, and the rules of composition of the old masters, who base everything around consonant chords, seem to them the effect of timidity and ignorance. Furthermore, as modal memory can hardly work when notes have harmonically false relations, melodies can have a significance only when overcrowded with chords and accents, until they completely disappear under a heap of modulations.

Still, it cannot be doubted that temperament has, along certain lines, brought out considerable developments in Western music. The newly invented modern piano was the means by which Chopin and Liszt could create an extraordinary number of new chords and modulations, and Wagner could not work without his Erard. This is because this instrument allowed composers to experiment, to search for chords that they could not imagine until they had heard them. And temperament, while disfiguring all the intervals of the major mode, also opened the door to a number of other modes. These, as we have already seen, were similarly disfigured, but no more so than the major mode.

Each note of the tempered scale and each tempered chord is open to numerous interpretations. The ear, of course, makes some sort of adaptation to find in it those correct intervals it can appreciate, but these adaptations can be widely different. Through this strange back door numerous modes and intervals that classical music had totally ignored have unknowingly appeared again in modern Western music. It goes without saying that if these modes and intervals were played correctly instead of being tempered, their beauty and expressiveness would be considerably intensified.

When this music, conceived on the piano, is to be played by an orchestra, however, a new difficulty appears: that of notation. The chords of the piano have introduced into music new intervals that accommodate themselves in some way or other to temperament. But if those chords are to be played on untempered instruments just as they are written, the result may be completely discordant. This is the case with Wagner, for example, whose music, conceived on the piano, was much more dissonant in his time, when the musicians of the orchestra made some distinction between sharps and flats, than it is nowadays when practically all musicians play in the tempered scale. The reason is that here the correct notes are no longer expressed by the written notation, and to play correctly would be to play what would have been written had a more complete system of notation permitted a better analysis.

This brings us to the observation that Western musical notation is of such imprecision that all sorts of misunderstandings are possible. Thus musicians speak of a sharp a little higher, of a third a little larger, of a brilliant-toned or a dull-toned note, in order to be able to achieve by instinct intervals whose significance is clearly distinct, whose definitions could be found, and that are even often implied in the principles of music as described in treatises on harmony, but that Western musical notation has no way of indicating. Such imprecision in notation also explains the misrepresentation of ancient modes and Asian melodies when they are written in Western notation, not to mention Western folk music, which is also completely disfigured.

The failure of modern musicians to produce any effect when they play their transcriptions of Greek or Asian modes comes from the fact that they always approach them through temperament, which disfigures their intervals and flattens their coloring, reducing practically everything to the tempered chromatic mode. We should not forget that although it is comparatively easy to recognize a mode or melody we already know when it is played in its tempered approximation, it is extremely difficult, if not impossible, to imagine its color and expression if one has never heard its real intervals.

Unfortunately, instead of realizing the deficiencies of their own musical notation by contact with Greek or Asian modes, many Western musicians, aided by their convenient evolutionist prejudice, prefer comfortably to consider that these modes, which they are unable to play, are "primitive," are of little interest, and could add nothing to the achievements of modern Western music.

Chapter Eight

THE SCALE OF SOUNDS

*To what could we not attain could we but discover the
physical laws that would allow us to gather together,
in more or less great quantity and according to proportions
that remain to be found, a certain ethereal substance
that pervades the air and gives to us music as well as
light, the phenomena of vegetation as well as those of
animal life! Do you realize? By giving him instruments
far superior to those he has at present, these new laws
would give to the composer new powers, and maybe a
harmony prodigious in comparison with that which rules
music today.*

Honoré de Balzac, Gambara

The Need for a Scale of Sounds

For the comparative study of different musical systems, as well as for the correct
execution of each one, it is necessary to establish a scale of sounds that will allow
both a clear and accurate notation of all the usual intervals and an immediate
appreciation of their nature and relative value. With the help of an accurate
notation, the reproduction of the different scales on an appropriate instrument
becomes easy.

If we collect the intervals used in the different systems, we can see that
their number and their combinations are not unlimited in practice. We have
seen, while studying the theory of Indian music, that the number of acoustic
ratios having a distinct significance in relation to one tonic is only twenty-two.
But by the permutation of that tonic, or simply by the permutation of the ratios
between the different notes, the number of different sounds within one octave
is raised to fifty-three principal sounds, to which are added in certain systems
either six secondary ones, bringing the total division to sixty sounds, or twelve
quarter tones, giving a total division of sixty-six distinct sounds. This scale can
be identified with the scale of fifths if the Pythagorean comma (5.88 savarts) is
assimilated to the comma *diesis* (81/80 = 5.4 savarts), which means an approximation of one hundredth of a tone. This division is by no means arbitrary. It
corresponds to the ideal structure of the octave. This is why it can be established

on the basis of any one of the systems, either by the progressive raising of the notes in a series of modulations within the scale of Zarlino, or by the combinations and permutations of the intervals necessary for melodic expression in the Indian, Arab, or ancient Greek musicians' systems, or again, by the development of the Chinese scale of fifths. In each case we get the same number of divisions.

Many intervals that are musically identical can be expressed by slightly different ratios in the scale of fifths and in the scale of proportions. Such is the case for the major half tone and the apotome, which are two expressions of the same interval: one is the harmonic relation to the tonic 16/15 (major half tone), the other is the cyclic ratio 2187/2048 (apotome). Their significance—their *śruti*—is identical. Their measure in savarts is, for the major half tone, 28.03, and, for the apotome, 28.52, which means that their difference is scarcely one hundredth of a tone. The Pythagoreans, and later the Arab and Turkish theorists, for mathematical reasons always considered the cyclic interval as the correct one and the harmonic interval as an approximation. But musically it is the harmonic interval that is really used and that must therefore be considered as the correct one.

There are, however, some intervals whose difference is so slight that the ear cannot easily detect it but whose functional difference is important; such is the case for the limma (256/243 = 22.63 savarts) and its complement to the minor tone (135/128 = 28.12 savarts: 256/243 x 135/128 = 10/9). In practice, these two intervals are identical, but their function, as we saw in connection with Indian music, is different. According to the Indian theory, one of them, 135/128, is a melodic interval (i.e., the two notes that constitute it can be played one after the other) and contains two *śrutis*, while the other, the limma proper, 256/243, contains only one *śruti* and should therefore be considered only as a difference between intervals.

Three, the Cyclic Number, and Five, the Modal Number

To render the classification of intervals easier, we have represented certain intervals with the simpler ratios in which the numerical element seven appears. From the point of view of the symbolic significance of numbers and, consequently, from the point of view of physics, this is an error. In this world of five elements in which we live, no prime number higher than five can enter into the composition of the substance from which a melodic or harmonic relation is made. The Chinese system, the abstract scale of fifths, even refuses to go beyond the number three; all its intervals are expressed in terms of powers of two and three. The introduction of the factor of five gives us the harmonic scale, of which the characteristic intervals are the harmonic major sixth (5/3), the harmonic major third (5/4), the minor third (6/5), the major half tone (16/15 = 2^4/[3 x 5]), the minor half tone (25/24 = 5^2/[3 x 2^3]), the comma *diesis* (81/80 = 3^4/[2^4 x 5]), and so forth.

The number five "humanizes" music. It makes music the instrument of expression no longer of abstract prototypes but of a tangible reality. The introduction of any higher prime number would take us beyond this reality into dangerous regions that are not within the scope of our normal perceptions and understanding. Seven is the number of the heavenly worlds as well as that of the infernal regions, and we usually have no means of knowing to which side it may lead us.

The intervals that contain the element seven cannot be physically pleasant, being by definition beyond the limits of physical harmony; their magical effect too is normally beyond our control. Consequently, their use in music and its theory serves no useful purpose. We shall indicate some of them here merely as a reference and because they have been spoken of by many theorists past and present.

There is a fundamental difference between the numerical substance from which the intervals are made and their subsequent grouping according to certain numbers for symbolic representation. The substance from which an image is made is necessarily material and cannot be anything else. Even if this image is a mere gesture, it comes necessarily within the limitation of space—that is, of ether, the fifth element. But although it is material in its substance, this image can be used to represent things that are not within the limits of the elements.

In the case of sounds, therefore, the substance—that is, the numerical ratios from which the sounds take their existence—must be limited to the numbers that are those of nature, of physical reality. On the other hand, once the notes have been built on the basis of their natural ratios, they can be grouped according to nonphysical numbers and thus become the symbols or the images of supernatural reality. The seven-note scale is thus taken to symbolize the transcendental role of music.

The number five is the highest prime number used in harmonic intervals. Similarly, in the scale of fifths, we cannot go melodically beyond the fourth ascending or descending fifth, which is in either case the fifth sound. This leads naturally to the scale of nine sounds, which is the most extensive simple melodic scale possible in any music, scales of more than nine sounds being necessarily mixtures of scales.

In reality, the completely manifested scale has only seven sounds, because in the scale of fifths only three successive fifths remain within the limits of the third power, beyond which we go out of this world's extension. But because the fourth and the fifth can function as subsidiary tonics, this limit is pushed back by one more step. Thus appears the scale of nine sounds, the absolute basis of the structure of all music. When we build a series of four ascending and four descending fifths on the tonic, we obtain a series of nine sounds, which constitutes the first element of the universal harmonic scale.

The four ascending fifths are:

1) G (Pa) = 3/2

2) D (Re) = 9/8

3) A+ (Dha+) = 27/16

4) E+ (Ga+) = 81/64.

The next fifth would be:

5) B+ (Ni+) = 243/128 = 278.14 savarts.

This last fifth forms with C (Sa) a Pythagorean limma (256/243), which conflicts with the slightly larger and softer harmonic limma formed by the B+ (Ni+) whose ratio is 256/135 = 277.91 savarts, the origin of which is explained below. In the series of fifths, intervals beyond the fourth fifth (81/64) are, in theory as well as in practice, not acceptable harmonically.

The four descending fifths are:

1) F (Ma) = 4/3

2) $\overset{L+}{B}\flat$ (NiL+) = 16/9

3) $\overset{L}{E}\flat$ (GaL) = 32/27

4) $\overset{L}{A}\flat$ (DhaL) = 128/81.

The next fifth would be:

5) $\overset{L-}{D}\flat$ (ReL-) = 256/243 = 22.63 savarts.

Preferable to this last fifth is the slightly larger harmonic limma 135/128 = 23.12 savarts, which is the fourth fifth of the harmonic A (Dha) = 5/3.

In both the ascending and the descending series, the next fifth (the sixth fifth) would give the prohibited augmented fourth, F♯ (Ma tīvra).

The augmented fourth in the ascending series is

$\overset{L+}{F}\sharp$ (MaL+) = 729/512,

while the augmented fourth in the descending series is

$\overset{L-}{F}\sharp$ (MaL-) = 1024/729.

The interval between these two augmented fourths constitutes the Pythagorean comma ($3^{12}/2^{19}$), the extreme limit of physical harmonies.

If we now consider the simplest ratio in which the number five appears in the numerator, we find it to be the A natural (Dha) = 5/3. The four ascending fifths built on this A natural (śuddha Dha) are:

1) E (Ga) = 5/4

2) B (Ni) = 15/8

3) $\overset{L-}{F}\sharp$ (MaL-) = 45/32

4) $\overset{L-}{D}\flat$ (ReL-) = 135/128.

The next fifth would be B♭ (NiL-) = 1280/729. The four descending fifths are:

1) D– (Re–) = 10/9

2) G– (Pa–) = 40/27

3) C– (Sa–) = 160/81

4) F– (Ma–) = 320/243.

The simplest ratio in which the number five enters as denominator is the harmonic minor third: E♭ (Ga♭) = 6/5. The four ascending fifths built upon it are:

1) B♭ (Ni♭) = 9/5

2) F+ (Ma+) = 27/20

3) C+ (Sa+) = 81/80

4) G+ (Pa+) = 243/160.

The four descending fifths are:

1) A♭ (Dha♭) = 8/5

2) D♭ (Re♭) = 16/15

3) F♯ (MaL+) = 64/45

4) B+ (Ni+) = 256/135.

If to these two series we add the two series that contain the square of five, we have, on the basis respectively of

F♯ (Ma♭) = 36/25 and F♯ (Ma♯) = 25/18,

two further complementary series. Ascending from F♯ (Ma♭) we have:

1) D♭ (Re♭) = 27/25

2) A— (Dha—) = 81/50

3) E— (Ga—) = 243/200

4) B— (Ni—) = 729/400.

Descending from F♯ (Ma♭) we have:

1) B++ (Ni++) = 48/25

2) E++ (Ga++) = 32/25

3) A++ (Dha++) = 128/75

4) D+ (Re+) = 256/225.

Ascending from F♯ (Ma♯) we have:

1) D♭ (Re♯) = 25/24

2) A♭ (Dha♯) = 25/16

3) E♭ (Ga♯) = 75/64

4) B♭ (NiL-) = 225/128.

Descending from F♯ (Ma♯) we have

1) B– (Ni–) = 50/27

2) E– (Ga–) = 100/81

3) A– (Dha–) = 400/243

4) D— (Re—) = 800/729.

This completes the universal harmonic scale that we had already been using, and whose intervals are shown in figure 16.

We should note here that the cyclic scale is called the scale of fifths because its basic interval happens to be the fifth successive note of the modern diatonic scale. But this unimportant peculiarity, in a scale arbitrarily chosen as basic scale, does not imply that this interval in any way connected with the number five. This confusion has led to the complete failure of many recent attempts to

Figure 16. THE SEVEN SERIES OF FIFTHS

series	Sa — C	Re — D	Ga — E	Ma — F	Pa — G	Dha — A	Ni — B	Sa — C
+++ series	128/125 (-3)	144/125 (-1)	162/125 (1)	512/375 (-4)	192/125 (-2)	216/125 (0)		
++ series	27/25 (3)	256/225 (-2)	32/25 (0)	36/25 (2)		128/75 (-1); 81/50 (4)	48/25 (1); 256/135 (-1)	
+ series	81/80 (3); 16/15 (-2)	729/640 (5); 27/25 (1)	6/5 (0)	27/20 (2); 64/45 (-3)	243/160 (4)	8/5 (-1)	9/5 (1); 256/135 (-4)	
basic series	1/1 (0); 256/243 (-5)	9/8 (2)	81/64 (4); 32/27 (-3)	4/3 (-1)	3/2 (1)	27/16 (3); 128/81 (-4)	243/128 (5); 16/9 (-2)	2/1
- series	135/128 (4)	10/9 (-1)	5/4 (1); 100/81 (-2)	45/32 (3); 320/243 (-4)	40/27 (-2)	5/3 (0)	15/8 (2); 160/81 (-3)	
— series	25/24 (1)	75/64 (3); 800/729 (-4)		25/18 (0)	25/16 (2)	400/243 (0); 225/128 (4)	50/27 (-1)	
——— series		125/108 (0)	8000/6561	125/96; 375/256	125/81 (-1)	125/72 (1)	125/64 (2); 4000/2127 (-1)	

The notes in each series are one comma *diesis* (81/80) above or below the notes of the next series.

The basic notes of the series are respectively:

C (Sa) = 1 for the basic series

E♭ (Ga♭) = 6/5 for the + series, F♯ (Ma♭) = 32/25 for the ++ series, the theoretical A♯ (Dha♯) = 216/125 for the +++ series

A (Dha) = 5/3 for the - series, F♯ (Ma♯) = 25/18 for the — series, the theoretical D++ (Re++) = 125/108 for the ——— series.

The number placed under each ratio represents the rank of the note in its respective series of fifths.

explain the symbolism of scales and chords by considering the interval of the fifth as representative of the number five. In reality, the interval of the fifth corresponds to the number three, its ratio being 3/2, and nowhere in the scale of fifths does the numerical element five appear. The numerical element five is essentially represented by the minor and major thirds, whose respective ratios are 6/5 and 5/4.

Similarities between the Scale of Fifths and the Scale of Proportions

By the system of harmonic proportions, as well as by that of the scale of fifths, we obtain a division of the octave into fifty-three intervals. But those intervals do not coincide exactly, because the notes of the scale of fifths divide the octave regularly into Pythagorean commas, while the notes of the scale of proportions divide it into commas *diesis*, with a slight discontinuity at every half tone. The intervals of these two similar scales are expressed by different ratios, one using the exact cyclic ratios and the other the simpler harmonic ratios. In musical practice it is the harmonic ratios that are correct, but the question of differentiation can scarcely arise because these two ratios are so near to each other that it is almost impossible to differentiate them directly. It is nevertheless easy to recognize them by the implications of the system to which they belong. This means that although it is difficult to find out to which system each individual sound belongs, a succession of a few sounds will at once show whether the system is modal or cyclic.

But this unity in the structure of the scales of sounds, though it is inherent in the very nature of sounds (the different systems being only more or less approximate means to express in terms of gross reality the metaphysical principles of sound), does not mean by implication that the laws regulating the different systems can be identical, nor that we can go from one to the other without difficulty. The same note can play a completely different role in the different systems, as is the case of the fourth F (Ma), for example, which forms with the tonic an essential interval (4/3) in the modal system, but which in the cyclic system is only the fifty-second fifth and thus forms a very distinct relation. Even then the cyclic fourth is never absolutely correct. In a similar way, the sixth fifth, F♯ (*Ma tīvra*), is the tritone, which is an essential interval in the scale of fifths but has to be cautiously handled in modal music.

Furthermore, if the intervals are used melodically, small differences that appear insignificant in the scale of sounds may, added to one another, result in a difference of *śruti*. In other words, we can say that although the scales of the two systems have the same number of steps, the melodies will not use those steps in the same order.

Figure 17.   THE UNIVERSAL SCALE OF SOUNDS (53 harmonic or cyclic intervals + 12 quarter tones = 65 notes)

	Note	approx. savarts	Interval with C (Sa)	Harmonic Scale			Cyclic Scale		
				ratio with C (Sa)	exact savarts	frequency	serial number of fifth	ratio with C (Sa)	exact savarts
1	C (Sa)					512			
2	+	5	comma	81/80 (comma diesis)	5.40	518.4	12th	$3^{12}/2^{19}$	5.88
3	++	10	2 commas	128/125 (46/45)^{b}	10.30 (9.55)	524.88	24th	$3^{24}/2^{38}$	11.74
	¼	14	quarter tone	(30/31)	14.24	529.06			
4	♯	18	minor half tone	25/24	17.73	533.33	36th	$3^{36}/2^{57}$	17.61
5	L-	23	limma	256/243 (135/128)	22.63 (23.12)	569.33	48th	$3^{48}/2^{76}$	23.48
6	L+	28	major half tone	16/15 (2187/2048)	28.03 (28.52)	546.13	7th	$3^{7}/2^{11}$	28.52
7	♭	33	large half tone	27/25	33.42	552.96	19th	$3^{19}/2^{30}$	34.48
	¾	37	three-quarter tone	135/124	36.89	557.41			
8	—	41	small tone	800/729 (11/10)	40.36 (41.39)	561.85	31st	$3^{31}/2^{39}$	40.35
9	–	47	minor tone	10/9	45.76	568.88	43rd	$3^{42}/2^{68}$	46.12
10	D (Re)	51	major tone	9/8	51.14	576	2nd	$3^{2}/2^{3}$	51.14
11	+	56	large tone	256/225 (8/7)	56.07 (57.99)	583.2	14th	$3^{14}/2^{22}$	57.07
12	++	61		59,049/51,300 (15/13)	61.10 (62.15)	590.49	26th	$3^{26}/2^{41}$	62.89
	¼	65		93/80	65.39	595.2			

13	#	69	small minor third	75/64	68.88	600	38th	$3^{38}/2^{60}$	68.76
14	L	74	trihemitone	32/27	73.79	606.81	50th	$3^{50}/2^{79}$	74.63
15	b	79	minor third	6/5	79.18	614.4	9th	$3^{9}/2^{14}$	79.68
	3/4	83		75/62	82.67	619.35			
16	—	87		8000/6561 (243/200)	86.12 (84.58)	624.29	21st	$3^{21}/2^{33}$	85.53
17	-	92	small major third	100/81	91.51	632.1	33rd	$3^{33}/2^{2}$	91.42
18	E (Ga)	97	major third	5/4	96.91	640	45th	$3^{45}/2^{71}$	97.37
19	+	102	ditone	81/64 (19/15)	102.31 (102.66)	648	4th	$3^{14}/2^{22}$	102.31
20	++	107	large major third	32/25	107.21	655.36	16th	$3^{16}/2^{25}$	108.17
	1/4	111		31/24	111.15	661.33			
21	—	115		125/96	114.64	666.66	28th	$3^{28}/2^{44}$	114.04
22	-	120	small fourth	320/243	119.54	674.23	40th	$3^{40}/2^{63}$	119.91
23	F (Ma)	125	fourth	4/3	124.94	682.66	52nd	$3^{52}/2^{82}$	125.78
24	+	130	large fourth	27/20	130.36	691.2	11th	$3^{11}/2^{17}$	130.815
25	++	135		512/375 (2187/1600)	134.70 (135.73)	699.84	23rd	$3^{23}/2^{36}$	136.68
	1/4	139		62/45	139.18	705.42			
26	#	143	small augmented fourth	25/18	142.67	711.11	35th	$3^{35}/2^{55}$	142.55

[a] On the basis of the physicists' pitch, where C_4 (Sa) = 512 cycles per second, and A_3 (Dha) = 426.6 cycles.
[b] The ratios in parentheses are approximate.

| Note | | approx. savarts | Interval with C (Sa) | *Harmonic Scale* | | | *Cyclic Scale* | | |
				ratio with C (Sa)	exact savarts	frequency	serial number of fifth	ratio with C (Sa)	exact savarts
27	L-	148	harmonic tritone	45/32 (7/5)	148.06 (146.13)	720	47th	$3^{47}/2^{74}$	148.42
28	L+	153	cyclic tritone	64/45	152.97	728.17	6th	$3^{6}/2^{9}$	153.46
29	♭	158	large augmented fourth	36/25	158.36	736.88	18th	$3^{18}/2^{28}$	159.42
	$3/4$	162		90/62	161.85	743.22			
30	—	166		375/256 (19/13)	165.79 (164.81)	749.15	30th	$3^{30}/2^{47}$	165.19
31	–	171	small fifth	40/27	170.70	758.52	42nd	$3^{42}/2^{66}$	171.06
32	G (Pa)	176	fifth	3/2	176.06	768	1st	$3^{1}/2^{1}$	176.09
33	+	181	large fifth	243/160	181.49	777.6	13th	$3^{13}/2^{20}$	181.96
34	++	186		192/125 (19,683/12,800)	186.39 (187.82)	787.32	25th	$3^{25}/2^{39}$	187.83
	$1/4$	190		31/20	190.33	793.6			
35	♯	194	small diminished sixth	25/16	193.82	800	37th	$3^{37}/2^{58}$	193.70
36	L	199	diminished sixth	128/81 (19/12)	198.71 (199.67)	809.09	49th	$3^{49}/2^{77}$	199.57
37	♭	204	diminished sixth	8/5	204.12	819.2	8th	$3^{8}/2^{12}$	204.61
	$3/4$	208		50/31	207.61	825.8			
38	—	212		81/50	209.52	829.44	20th	$3^{20}/2^{31}$	210.47
39	–	217	small sixth	400/243	216.45	842.80	32nd	$3^{32}/2^{50}$	216.34

No.	Note		Ratio						
40	A (Dha)	222	5/3	harmonic sixth	221.85	853.33	44th	$3^{44}/2^{69}$	222.21
41	+	227	27/16	cyclic sixth	227.24	864	3rd	$3^{3}/2^{4}$	227.24
42	++	232	128/75 (12/7)	large sixth	232.15 (234.08)	874.76	15th	$3^{15}/2^{23}$	233.11
	1/4	236	31/18		236.09	882.33			
43	#	240	125/72	small minor seventh	239.58	888.88	27th	$3^{27}/2^{42}$	238.98
44	L-	245	225/128 (7/4)	seventh harmonic	244.99 (243.04)	900	39th	$3^{39}/2^{61}$	244.85
45	L+	250	16/9	minor seventh	249.88	910.22	51st	$3^{51}/2^{80}$	250.72
46	♭	255	9/5	minor seventh	255.27	921.6	10th	$3^{10}/2^{15}$	255.76
	3/4	259	29/16		258.28	928			
47	—	263	40,000/2187 (729/400)		262.21 (260.67)	936.44	22nd	$3^{22}/2^{34}$	261.62
48	–	268	50/27 (13/7)	small seventh	267.62 (268.84)	948.15	34th	$3^{34}/2^{53}$	267.49
49	B (Ni)	273	15/8	major seventh	273.99	960	46th	$3^{46}/2^{72}$	273.36
50	+	278	243/128 (256/135)	cyclic major seventh	278.40 (277.91)	972	5th	$3^{5}/2^{7}$	278.40
51	++	283	48/25	large major seventh	283.31	983.04	17th	$3^{17}/2^{26}$	284.26
	1/4	287	60/31 (31/16)		286.79 (287.24)	990.96			
52	—	291	125/64		290.73	1000	29th	$3^{29}/2^{45}$	290.13
53	–	296	160/81	small octave	295.63	1012.5	41st	$3^{41}/2^{64}$	296.00
1	C (Sa)	301	2/1	octave	301.03	1024	53rd	$3^{53}/2^{83}$	301.84

Remarks on the Scale of Sounds

The division of the octave into fifty-three intervals, in the harmonic and the cyclic systems, is given in figure 17. The frequencies are given according to the scale of the physicists: C (Sa) = powers of two, A_3 (Dha) = 426.6 Hz. To obtain the French pitch (A = 435), the scale must be raised by more than one comma; for the American high pitch (A = 453), the scale should be raised by a little over one limma.

If we want to experiment with all the theoretical intervals indicated by the ancient Greek physicists, these intervals can, with a sufficiently close approximation, be replaced by the neighboring intervals of the scale presented here without having their expression perceptibly disfigured. This scale plays a role opposite to that of temperament in regard to the scale of the Greek physicists; that is to say, it brings the intervals back to their harmonic prototype, while temperament disharmonizes the harmonic sounds. Furthermore, most of the intervals invented by the physicists are interesting only as attempts to represent the true intervals, their ratios often being meaningless by themselves. According to Indian theory, all the sounds contained in the twenty-second part of an octave have the same general expressive quality, and are differentiated only by more or less fullness and intensity.

In musical practice, the following assimilations are acceptable:

1) The comma *diesis*, 81/80 (5.4 savarts), can be assimilated to the Pythagorean comma, $3^{12}/2^{19}$ (5.88 savarts).

2) The double comma, 128/125 (10.3 savarts), can be assimilated to 46/45 (9.55 savarts), 6561/6400 (10.79 savarts), 512/499 (11.17 savarts), 499/486 (11.46 savarts), and 250/243 (12.33 savarts).

3) The quarter tone (14 savarts) can be assimilated to 31/30 (14.84 savarts) and 32/31 (13.79 savarts).

4) The minor half tone, 25/24 (17.73 savarts), can be assimilated to ratios between 28/27 (51.8 savarts) and 24/23 (18.48 savarts).

5) The limma, 256/243 (22.63 savarts), can be assimilated to 20/19 (22.30 savarts) and to 135/128 (23.12 savarts).

6) The major half tone, 16/15 (28.03 savarts), can be assimilated to the apotome, 2187/2048 (28.52 savarts).

7) The large half tone, 27/25 (33.32 savarts), can be assimilated to 14/13 (32.19 savarts).

As we have seen, the limma (256/243) is properly speaking merely the complement of the apotome (2187/2048) within the major tone (9/8). It is therefore a complementary interval in the ascending scale, but a direct interval in the descending (ancient) one. An interval of one limma separates C (Sa) from

B+ (Ni+), which is the fifth fifth of the cyclic series; the same interval separates the second fifth D (Re) from the seventh fifth C♯ (ReL+). This is because a difference of five fifths always produces a limma. In the ascending scale is found the limma 135/128 (23.12 savarts), which is equivalent to the forty-eighth fifth (23.48 savarts).

To study and produce all these different intervals, and to accustom the ear to them, it is necessary to have an instrument allowing their accurate execution.[1] The simplest is, of course, a stringed instrument of sufficient dimensions, such as the Indian *sitār*, with easily movable frets and with the exact place of the *śrutis* marked along the slide on which the frets move. To mark these places we should remember that the string length ratios refer to the string shortened without pulling or pressing. If the finger presses the string on the fret, the tension is increased and therefore the place of the fret must be accordingly corrected. This rectification is easy to do by tuning two strings in unison at the correct pitch. One of the strings is then lightly pinched with light wood or metal tongs, without pulling or pressing it, leaving free the portion of string corresponding to the desired note. The fret is then adjusted until the second string, pressed upon the fret, comes into perfect unison with the first string. A mark is then made on the wood so that the fret may be easily and exactly replaced whenever the same note is desired. This must be done for each note of the scale, so that the whole length of the instrument becomes marked and by changing the place of the frets the correct tuning for each mode can be obtained.

Conclusions

We have found that according to traditional data as well as experimental facts:

1) The division of the octave into fifty-three intervals is in conformity with the nature of sounds.

2) The intervals used in all music and at all times are only the major tone, the minor tone, the major half tone (apotome), and the limma, together with the intervals resulting from their sum or difference (the minor half tone, for example, is the difference of the minor tone and the major half tone). These, by their different combinations, produce the scale of fifty-three sounds.

3) Any other intervals would not bring out a distinct expressive quality, and would in any case be less consonant. Their use is therefore without interest.

4) Within one octave we cannot discern more than twenty-two groups of sounds having distinct expressive qualities. The division of the octave into fifty-three intervals is only necessary to make these twenty-two different expressions coincide with perfect harmonic relations in the different modes.

5) All twenty-two divisions cannot be used simultaneously in a mode, or in any melodic or harmonic combination. At the most twelve, and at the least three notes are used, the normal number being seven.

In all the traditional modal systems, the intervals used musically are the same. The various divisions of the octave differ only because some methods take into account a greater number of intervals. Thus the notes of the pentatonic scale are five of the notes of the heptatonic scale, which can in turn be identified with seven of the degrees of the twelve-note scale, which are themselves twelve of the notes of the Arabic division into seventeen notes, which are identical to seventeen of the twenty-two *śrutis*, all of which which belong to the scale of fifty-three sounds. This scale can further be extended up to sixty sounds, beyond which we are no longer within the field of music.

REFERENCES

Chapter 1

1. *Paradiso*, 1.103.
2. Quoted by Préau (1932).
3. Guénon (1936), p. 68.
4. Préau (1935), p. 350.
5. Saraswatī.
6. Woodroffe, p. 77.
7. Ibid., p. 210.
8. Ibid., p. 209.
9. René Guénon, in an article on the language of birds, explains: "The (Vedic) hymns were given the name of *chandahs*, a word that properly means 'rhythm.' The same idea is contained also in the word *dhikr*, which in Islamic esotericism applies to rhythmic formulas exactly corresponding to the Hindu *mantras*. The purpose of the repetition of such formulas is to produce a harmonization of diverse elements of being and to establish vibrations able, by their repercussion across the series of stages in indefinite hierarchy, to open some communication with superior stages, which is, as a rule, the essential and primordial purpose of every rite" (Guénon, "La Langue des oiseaux," p. 670).
10. Woodroffe, p. 77.
11. Fabre d'Olivet, p. 24.
12. Lebaisquais, p. 492.
13. Michael Maier thus divides the octave into sixty intervals, as do the Chinese, in conformity with the traditional division of the scale of fifths.
14. Quoted by Chacornac, p. 461.

15. Guénon (Feb. 1937), p. 75.

16. Rules from the *Han*. The *lü* are sound tubes, of rigorously accurate dimensions, which are used as gauges for the measurement of sounds.

17. Vuilliaud, p. 105.

18. *Paradiso*, 1.106.

19. Argos, p. 702.

20. We can see here that the number twelve represents an area and not a sequence.

21. Fabre d'Olivet, pp. 59–60.

22. de Mengel, p. 494.

23. Coomaraswamy (1937), p. 53n.

24. Lebasquais, p. 493. The *Yue ji* is a music book compiled in the time of Wu Di (147–87 B.C.E.) that includes extracts from the *Zhou gwan*.

25. Guénon, "Les Arts," p. 134.

26. Throughout this book, we shall use two systems for naming the notes of the various scales studied: the Western system (C, D, E, F, G, A, B) and the Indian system (Sa, Re, Ga, Ma, Pa, Dha, Ni). We shall, by convention, assimilate Sa to C.

27. Quoted by Courant, pp. 206–7.

Chapter 2

1. Yekta Bey, p. 2953n.

2. Gounod.

3. Gevaert (1903), p. 177.

4. Courant, p. 88.

5. Gastoué.

6. Emmanuel (1924).

7. Gevaert (1903).

8. If in a given mode, without changing any of the notes, we start the scale from a note other than the original tonic, the scale thus obtained is called a *plagal* form of the original mode.

9. A striking difference between the structure of the cyclic system and that of the modal system is that the one normally forms an ascending scale and the other normally a descending one. This allows us to distinguish at first sight to which family a system originally belonged. Since by its very structure the cycle of fifths forms an ascending series, the intermediary notes between the tones of each tetrachord will be sharpened (*tīvra*). On the other hand, modes normally form descending scales, and so the interme-

diate notes will be flattened (*komal*). This can be seen in Indian and Chinese music, respectively.

10. Fabre d'Olivet, p. 80.

11. Dubrochet.

12. Willard, p. 55.

13. Rousseau was mistaken when he asserted that Europeans are the only people who possess harmony and chords; polyphony was practiced in many countries a very long time before it was heard in Europe. Chinese and classical Javanese music, for example, are essentially polyphonic, although it is interesting to note that they are among the less refined and delicate of the Eastern systems, and Chinese music has often been described as a pleasure more for the mind than for the ear.

14. Rousseau.

15. Fabre d'Olivet, p. 16.

16. Jones, p. 128.

17. Ibid., p. 127.

Chapter 3

1. The French physicist Savart (1791–1841) advocated this system, to which his name was given.

2. al-Fārābī.

3. Yekta Bey.

4. Quintilianus, p. 3.

Chapter 4

1. Courant.

2. Ibid.

3. *Yo ki*, quoted by Courant.

4. Zu Xiaosun, quoted by Courant.

5. Courant.

6. *Yo ki*, quoted by Courant.

7. Pao Ye (fl. c. 77 C.E.), quoted by Courant.

8. See *Orient et occident*, by René Guénon, p. 70n: "[Fu Xi's] exact date is 3468 B.C.E., according to a chronology based on the exact description of the condition of the sky at the time. Let us add that the name of Fu Xi is used in reality as a designation for a whole period of Chinese history."

9. Courant.

10. Quoted by Matgioi, p. 168.

11. *Yo ki*, quoted by Courant.

12. Emperor Xiao Wen (477–99 C.E.), quoted by Courant.

13. Courant.

14. Ibid.

15. Among the musical terms that met with some change of meaning in their passage from Sanskrit to Chinese can be noted the Sanskrit *pañchama* (fifth note), which becomes in Chinese *banzhan* but is used for the sixth note, and the Sanskrit *rishabha*, meaning "a bull" and representing the second (ascending) degree, which becomes in Chinese *xulizha*, meaning "sound of the bull" and representing the seventh degree, or second descending degree. Instruments were also imported into China from India and Persia, such as the Indian *tambura*, which the Chinese call *tabula*, or the Persian *sitār*, which becomes *satuoer*.

16. "Which implies that four, immediately produced by three, is in a certain way equivalent to the entire set of numbers; and this is so because, as soon as we have the quaternary, we also have, by the addition of the four first numbers, the denary, which represents the complete numerical cycle: 1 + 2 + 3 + 4 = 10. This is the Pythagorean *tetractys*" (Guénon [1937], p. 75).

17. Courant.

18. Nicholas Mercator and Holder established a system of temperament of fifty-three degrees on this basis.

19. The Pythagorean great year is one fifth of the Chinese great year or *yuen*, which is equal to 29.920 x 5 = 129,600 years, and is itself double the Indian *manvantara*, 25,920 x 2 1/2 = 64,800 years, which according to Eastern doctrine always brings humanity back to its starting point. The duration of this complete evolution is thus two and a half precessions of the equinoxes.

20. Zheng Xuan, quoted by Courant.

21. Courant.

22. Experiments during the Han period, quoted by Courant.

23. Decree of Yang Jian, 590 C.E.

24. Quoted by Chavannes, 3.636.

25. Courant.

26. Levis, p. 67.

27. D'Olivet, p. 73.

28. Though indistinguishable in its Western transliteration from the other form of *lü*, this is in fact a different word, represented by a different Chinese character.

29. Courant.

30. "Yellow is the color of the natural agent earth (*tu*), that is, of the base, of fixity, of the center, of the pole around which revolutions are accomplished."

31. Courant.

32. Ibid.

33. Ibid.

34. From a report made by Wang Po in 959 C.E., quoted by Courant.

35. Zu Xiaosun, quoted by Courant.

36. *Da king hui dian* (eighteenth century), quoted by Courant.

37. Prince Caiyu (sixteenth century), quoted by Courant.

38. Courant.

39. Ibid.

40. Ibid.

41. Ibid.

42. *Yue ji*, quoted by Courant.

43. *Yo ki*, quoted by Courant.

44. See Préau (1932), p. 556.

45. Courant.

46. Ibid.

47. Ibid.

48. Ibid.

49. David and Lussy, pp. 17–36.

Chapter 5

1. Rāmāmātya, 2.7–9.

2. Śārngadeva, 1.22–23.

3. Tagore (1874), p. 340.

4. Saraswatī, p. 3.

5. Ibid.

6. These elemental principles must not be imagined, like the elements of modern Western science, to be definite chemical substances or states of such substances (liquid, solid, etc.). All chemical substances are a combination of the five elements, though their relative proportion may vary. René Guénon explains that "the cause of sound abides in the ether, but it must be understood that this cause is to be differentiated from the various media that can be used secondarily for the propagation of sound. . . . The sound quality is also perceptible in the four other elements insofar as they

all proceed from ether" (Guénon, "La Théorie hindoue," p. 327).

7. "[That sound is produced] by vibratory movement . . . is far from being a recent discovery, as some might believe; Kanāda expressly declares that 'sound is propagated by undulations, wave after wave, radiating in all directions from a definite center.' Sound . . . is the least differentiated of all movements because of its 'isotropism.' And this is why it can give birth to all the other movements, which will be differentiated from it in that they will no longer be uniform nor spread in all directions. . . . Thus ether . . . has for its origin an elementary movement produced from an initial point in this limitless cosmic medium . . . this is nothing other than the prototype of the sound wave. The sense of hearing, moreover, is the only one that allows us to perceive directly a vibratory movement, even if we admit, with most modern physicists, that the other sensations originate from a transformation of similar movements" (ibid., p. 327).

8. Like Plato, Indian philosophers consider ideas as eternal prototypes having an independent existence by themselves, thought being only the perception of those ideas.

9. Saraswatī.

10. Tagore (1874), p. 340.

11. Simultaneously issued from the primordial creative sound, the divisions of articulate sound and of musical sound (śabda and svara) are strictly parallel and interdependent. The very terms that express these divisions are often identical.

12. "It appears that the West owes its system of naming notes by the initial letters of their names to Indian music; they borrowed it, like their system of numbers, from the Arabs, who learned it from the Indians" (Lévi).

13. Bhārata, 28.69.

14. Saraswatī.

15. Rāmāmātya, p. 61.

16. Coomaraswamy (1933), p. 111.

17. Bhārata, 27.22.

18. Willard.

19. The octave is divided into twenty-two intervals, called śrutis; the major tone contains four śrutis, the minor tone three śrutis, and the half tone two śrutis.

20. Bhārata, 28.21.

21. Bhārata, 28.22.

22. Euclid, Elements, book 13, sixth proposition.

23. The two accessory sounds cannot be taken as the tonic of a scale.

24. See Framjee, p. 71.

25. For an interpretation of a few of these, see Framjee, pp. 33–107.

26. Bhārata, 28.22.

27. Guénon, *L'Esotérisme de Dante*, p. 66.

28. al-Fārābī, p. 25.

29. Ibid., p. 253.

30. Hildephonse.

31. Saint Augustine, *De ritualis ecclesias ad sannar*, 119.

32. Plutarch.

33. See Safiyu-d-Dīn, p. 127, and al-Fārābī, p. 243.

34. Tagore (1874), p. 360.

35. On tempered instruments these different feelings will become clear only when the structure of the underlying chord imposes the interpretation of the particular third either as a harmonic third or as a ditone. Tempered instruments can therefore be used only for harmonic music, provided the structure of the chords is specially built to make up for their deficiencies, but their use in modal music is impossible because the feeling of the notes remains indeterminate and therefore without appeal.

36. More ancient works such as the *Sangīta makaranda* use different names and start from another tonic. Many questions have been raised concerning the interpretation of the *śrutis* as given by Śārngadeva, because of the change of tonic that has since taken place. As we are attempting to give only a general idea of the method through which the study of scales should be approached, we cannot enter here into a discussion of such difficult questions, which are dealt with at length in my *Sémantique musicale*.

37. Framjee, p. 24.

38. "They do not pretend that those minute intervals (*śrutis*) are equal, but consider them as equal in practice" (Jones).

39. See d'Erlanger, 1.138.

40. Clements.

41. Yekta Bey, p. 2950.

42. See Rouanet, p. 2715.

43. Jones, p. 134.

44. Grosset (1924).

45. Ibid.

46. Professor Weber believes that the French *gamme* and the English *gamut*

are derived from the Sanskrit *grāma* (Prakrit *gama*), and he sees therein direct proof of the Indian origin of the Western scale of seven notes. According to him, it would have come from India through the Arabs and the Persians. The Arab word for scale, *Jamā ah*, pronounced in certain provinces *Gama ah*, seems to confirm this theory. See Weber; Grosset (1924), p. 292; and d'Erlanger, 2.312.

47. This is one of the reasons why the corresponding mode of the modern diatonic scale, the mode of C (Sa), the Western major mode or Indian *rāga Bilaval that*, was prohibited in Europe in ancient times and until the end of the Middle Ages.

48. Ahobala.

49. *Politics*, 5.5.8.

50. Śārngadeva, p. 264.

51. The use in Indian music of the augmented fourth, or tritone, at the critical times of midnight and midday reminds us of the magical importance attached to those hours, and of the use of the tritone (*diabolus in musica*) by Western musicians for the representation of magic, which is nothing other than the possible intersection, at certain critical hours, of worlds that cannot normally communicate. It is used conspicuously in this way by Schumann for the character of Manfred, by Wagner every time a magician appears, by Berlioz in the *Symphonie fantastique*, by Weber in *Der Freischutz*, and so on. In Chinese music the *lü rui bin*, corresponding to the augmented fourth, represents the summer solstice, the critical moment in the annual cycle when the masculine influx, hot and creative, gives place to the feminine influx, cold and destructive.

52. For its correspondence with the scale of fifths, see chapter 8.

Chapter 6

1. d'Erlanger, p. 590.
2. Yekta Bey, p. 2958.
3. Rivaud, p. 43.
4. Ibid., pp. 45–47.
5. Emmanuel, p. 418.
6. d'Erlanger, 2.578.
7. Emmanuel, p. 418.
8. Ibid.
9. Ibid., p. 417.
10. Yekta Bey.
11. Quintilianus.

12. al-Fārābī, p. 97.

13. Emmanuel, p. 444.

Chapter 7

1. Only scales and modes come within the scope of this book. As these are greatly simplified today in the West, modern Western music will have only a small place in this work. The modal division of the scale as applied to the study of the significance of chords will not be dealt with here, but is covered in more detail in my *Sémantique musicale*.

2. *Timaeus*.

3. Fabre d'Olivet, p. 41 (my italics).

4. Gastoué.

5. Fabre d'Olivet, p. 42.

6. Ibid., p. 87.

7. Fabre d'Olivet, p. 41.

8. Britt.

9. Blaserna and Helmholtz, p. 120.

10. Langel, p. 154.

11. Courant, p. 90.

Chapter 8

1. In accordance with the scale of sounds described herein, Stephan Kudelski, the designer of the Nagra tape recorder, constructed a prototypical instrument, the S 52, capable of playing fifty-two divisions of the octave with absolute precision. Another instrument, the Semantic, also based on Daniélou's scale of sounds, is currently being developed by two French technicians, Michel Geiss and Christian Braut. Whereas the S 52 was conceived mainly for the study and measurement of intervals, the Semantic is designed for the performance of musical compositions exploiting the resources of the scale of sounds. —*Editor*

BIBLIOGRAPHY

Ahobala. *Sangīta-parijāta*. In Sanskrit. Calcutta, 1884.

al-Fārābī. *Kitābu i-mūsīqī al-kabīr*. French translation by d'Erlanger. Paris: Paul Geuthner, 1939.

Amiot, Père. *De la musique des chinois tant anciens que modernes*. Mémoires concernant les chinois, vol. 6. Paris, 1780.

Argos. "Dante et l'hermétisme." *Voile d'Isis*. Paris, 1931.

Augustine, Saint. *De ritualis ecclesias ad sannar*. Fifth century.

Avicenna (Abū Ali al-Husayn ibn Abd-Allāh ibn Sīna). *Kitâbu ash-shifâ*. French translation by d'Erlanger. Paris: Paul Geuthner, 1935.

Avitus. "Notes sur le yī kīng." *Voile d'Isis*. Paris, 1931.

Basu, Śivendranāth. *Sangīta samuchchaya*. In Hindi. Banaras: Bhārata Kalā Parishada, 1924.

———. *Sangīta-praveshikā*. In English and Hindi. Banaras: Banaras Hindu University, n.d.

Bhārata. *Natya-śāstra*. In Sanskrit. Banaras: Vidya Vilas Press, 1929.

Bhatkhande, Pandit Vishnu Nārāyan. *Hindusthani-sangīta-paddhati*. In Hindi. Bombay, 1937.

Biot, Edward. *Le Tchéou li ou rites des Tchéou*. French translation from the Chinese. 3 vols. Paris, 1851.

Blaserna and Helmholtz. *Le son et la musique*.

Boethius. *De musica*. Sixth century.

Bosanquet, R. H. M. "On the Hindu Division of the Octave." *Proceedings of the Royal Society* (London, 1877). Reproduced in Tagore (1882).

Bouasse, H. *Acoustique générale*. Paris: Delagrave, 1926.

Bourgault-Ducoudray, L. A. "Etudes sur la musique ecclésiastique grecque." In *Mission musicale en Grèce et en Orient, janvier–mai 1875*. Paris: Hachette, 1877.

Britt, Ernest. *La synthèse de la musique*. Paris: Vega, n.d.

Burnell, A. C. *The "Arsheyabrahmana" of the Sāmaveda*. Sanskrit text with an introduction and index to words. Bangalore, 1876.

Callias, Hélène de. *Magie sonore*. Paris: Vega, 1938.

Chacornac, Paul. "Michel Maier." *Voile d'Isis* no. 150–51 (Paris, June–July 1932).

Chavannes, Edouard. *Les mémoires historiques de Se-ma Ts'ien*. French annotated translation. Paris, 1895.

Clements, E. *Introduction to the Study of Indian Music*. London: Longman, Green, 1913.

Coomaraswamy, A. K. *A New Approach to the Vedas*. London: Luzac, 1933.

———. *The Transformation of Nature in Art*. Cambridge, Mass.: Harvard University Press, 1935.

———. "Beauté, lumière et son." *Etudes traditionnelles* no. 206 (Paris, February 1937).

Courant, Maurice. "Chine et Corée, essai historique sur la musique classique des chinois." In *Encyclopédie de la musique et dictionnaire du Conservatoire*. Paris: Delagrave, 1922.

Daniélou, Alain. *Sémantique musicale*. Paris: Hermann, 1978.

———. *The Rāgas of Northern Indian Music*. London: Barrie and Rockliff, 1968; New Delhi: Munshiram Manoharlal, 1980.

David and Lussy. *Histoire de la notation musicale depuis ses origines*. Paris: Imprimerie Nationale, 1882.

de Mengel, G. *Voile d'Isis* (Paris, 1929): 494.

d'Erlanger, Baron Rodolphe. *La musique arabe*. 3 vols. Paris: Paul Geuthner, 1930.

Dubrochet, H. *Mémoires sur une nouvelle théorie de l'harmonie*. Paris, 1840.

Emmanuel, Maurice. "Grèce, art gréco-romain." In *Encyclopédie de la musique et dictionnaire du Conservatoire*. Paris: Delagrave, 1924.

———. *Le tyran ut* (unpublished).

Fabre d'Olivet. *La musique expliquée comme science et comme art*. Paris: Jean Pinasseau, 1928. English translation by Joscelyn Godwin, *Music Explained as Science and Art*. Rochester, Vt.: Inner Traditions International, 1989.

Fétis, F. J. *Histoire générale de la musique*. Paris, 1869.

Fox Strangways, A. H. *Music of Hindosthan*. Oxford: Clarendon Press, 1914.

Framjee, Pandit Firoze. *Theory and Practice of Indian Music.* Poona, 1938.

Gastoué, Amédée. "La musique byzantine et le chant des églises d'orient." In *Encyclopédie de la musique et dictionnaire du Conservatoire.* Paris: Delagrave, 1924.

Gevaert, François-Auguste. *L'histoire et la théorie de la musique dans l'antiquité.* 2 vols. Ghent, 1875, 1881.

———. *Problèmes musicaux d'Aristote.* Ghent, 1903.

———. *Mélopée antique.* Ghent, n.d.

Ghyka, Matila C. *Esthétique des proportions dans la nature et dans les arts.* Paris: Gallimard, 1927.

———. *Le nombre d'or.* Paris: Gallimard, 1931.

Gounod, Charles. Article in *Le ménestrel* (Paris, 22 February 1882).

Grosset, Joanny. *Bhâratîya-nâtya-çastram, traité de Bharata sur le théâtre.* Sanskrit text, French critical edition. Paris: Leroux, 1888.

———. *Contribution à l'étude de la musique hindoue.* Paris: Leroux, 1888.

———. "Inde, histoire de la musique depuis l'origine jusqu'à nos jours." In *Encyclopédie de la musique et dictionnaire du Conservatoire.* Paris: Delagrave, 1924.

Guénon, René. *Orient et occident.* Paris: Didier et Richard, 1930.

———. "La langue des oiseaux." *Voile d'Isis* no. 143 (Paris, November 1931).

———. *Le symbolisme de la croix.* Paris: Vega, 1931.

———. "Les arts et leur conception traditionnelle." *Voile d'Isis* no. 184 (Paris, 1935): 134.

———. "Remarques sur la notation mathématique." *Voile d'Isis* no. 184 (Paris, April 1935).

———. "La théorie hindoue des cinq éléments." *Voile d'Isis* nos. 188–89 (Paris, 1935): 327.

———. "Quelques aspects du symbolisme du poisson." *Etudes traditionnelles* no. 104 (Paris, February 1936).

———. "Remarques sur la notation mathématique." *Etudes traditionnelles* nos. 205–7 (Paris, January–March, 1937).

———. *L'ésotérisme de Dante.* 2nd edition. Paris: Editions Traditionnelles, 1939.

———. *Le roi du monde.* 2nd edition. Paris: Editions traditionnelles, 1939.

Helmholtz, H. *Théorie physiologique de la musique, fondée sur l'étude des sensations auditives.* Translated from the German by G. Guéroult. Paris: Masson, 1868.

———. *see also* Blaserna and Helmholtz.

Hildephonse, Bishop. "De pane eucharistico." *Posthumous Works of Mabillon,* vol. 1. Paris, n.d.

Jones, Sir William. "On the Musical Modes of the Hindus." *Asiatic Researches* (Calcutta, 1792). Reproduced in Tagore (1874).

Krishna Rao, H. P. *The Psychology of Music*. Bangalore, 1923.

Kṣemarāja. *Commentaries on Shiva Sûtra Vimarshinî*. Sanskrit Kashmir Series, vol. 1. Srinagar, 1911. French translation by André Préau, *Voile d'Isis* nos. 188–9 (Paris, August–September 1935).

Laloy, Louis. *Aristoxène de Tarente et la musique de l'antiquité*. Paris, 1904.

Langel, A. *La voix, l'oreille et la musique*. Paris: Germer-Baillière, 1887.

Lebasquais, Elie. "Tradition hellénique et art grec." *Voile d'Isis* no. 192 (Paris, December 1935).

Lévi, Sylvain. *Le théâtre indien*. Paris: Bouillon, 1890.

———. "Inde." *Grande encyclopédie*. Paris, n.d.

Levis, J. H. *Chinese Musical Art*. Beijing: Henri Vetch, 1936.

Mansfield, O. A. *The Student's Harmony*. London: Weekes, 1896.

Matgioi. *La voie métaphysique*. Paris: Chacornac, 1905. Paris, 1936.

Nārada. *Nārada-śikshā*. In Sanskrit. Banaras Sanskrit Series, Banaras, 1893.

Ouseley, Sir W. "An Essay on the Music of Hindustan." *Oriental Collections* (London, 1797–1800). Reprinted in Tagore (1874).

Plutarque (Plutarch). *Isis et Osiris*. Translated by Mario Meunier. Paris: L'Artisan du Livre, 1924.

Popley, H. A. *The Music of India*. Calcutta: Associated Press; London: Curwen, 1921.

Préau, André. "La fleur d'or." *Voile d'Isis* (Paris, 1931).

———. "Lie Tseu." *Voile d'Isis* nos. 152–3 (Paris, August–September 1932).

———. "Le secret des mantras, commentaires sur le Shiva Sutrâ Vimarshinî (de Kshemarāja)." *Voile d'Isis* nos. 188–9 (Paris, August–September 1935).

Quintilianus, Aristides. *De musica*. Meibom, Germany, n.d.

Rāmāmātya. *Svaramela-kalānidhi*. Sanskrit text and translation by M. S. Ramaswami Aiyar. Annamalai University, South India, 1932.

Rivaud, Albert. "Notice et traduction du *Timée*." In *Platon, œuvres complètes*. Paris: Les Belles Lettres, 1925.

Rouanet, Jules. "La musique arabe." *Encyclopédie de la musique et dictionnaire du Conservatoire*. Paris: Delagrave, 1922.

Rousseau, Jean-Jacques. *Dictionnaire de la musique*. Paris, 1747.

Roy, Hemedra Lal. *Problems of Hindustani Music*. Calcutta: Bharati Bhāvan, 1937.

Safiyu-d-Dīn Al-Urmawī. *Aśśarafiyyah* and *Kitāb al-adwār*. French translation by d'Erlanger. Paris: Paul Geuthner, 1938.

Saraswatī, Swāmī Hariharānand. "Śabda and Artha." In Hindi. *Siddhānt*, 1.45 (Banaras, 1941).

Śārngadeva. *Sangīta-ratnākara*. In Sanskrit, with Kallinātha's commentary. Poona: Ānandāshram, 1897.

Séraphin Lecouvreur. *Le cheu king*. Chinese text with translation into Latin and French. Ho Kien Fou, 1896.

———. *Chou king*. Chinese text with translation into Latin and French. Ho Kien Fou, 1897.

———. *Li ki, ou mémoires sur les bienséances*. 2 vols. Ho Kien Fou, 1906.

Somanātha. *Rāga-vibodha*. In Sanskrit. Lahore, 1901.

Tagore, Sourindro Mohun. *Hindu Music*. Reprinted from the *Hindoo Patriot* (Calcutta, 1874).

———. *Hindu Music from Various Authors*. 2nd ed. Calcutta, 1882.

Vishnu Digambar, Pandit. *Rāga-praveśa*. In Hindi. Bombay, 1921.

Vuilliaud, Paul. "La tradition pythagoricienne." *Voile d'Isis* nos. 170–1 (Paris, February–March 1934).

Weber, A. "Indische literarische Geschichte" and "Indische Studien." Translated from the German by John Mann and Theodor Zachariae. In *The History of Indian Literature*. London: Trübner, 1882.

Widor, C. M. *Initiation musicale*. Paris: Hachette, 1923.

Willard, N. A. *Of Harmony and Melody*. Reproduced in Tagore (1874).

Woodroffe, Sir John. *The Garland of Letters* (Varnamala). In *Studies in the Mantra Shāstra*. Madras: Ganesh; London: Luzac, 1922.

Yekta Bey, Raouf. "La musique turque." In *Encyclopédie de la musique*. Paris: Delagrave, 1922.

INDEX

*Explore the spiritual dimension of music in other
titles from Inner Traditions...*

HARMONY OF THE SPHERES
The Pythagorean Tradition in Music
Joscelyn Godwin • 0-89281-265-6 • $29.95 hardcover

Most people have heard the phrase "harmony of the spheres" without really knowing what it means. This book traces the history of the idea that the whole cosmos, with its circling planets and stars, is in some way a harmonious or musical entity. Godwin, a professor of music at Colgate University, draws on classical, Christian, Jewish, and Muslim sources, as well as the rich esoteric tradition of modern France, and he brings together the writings of Giorgi, Kepler, Fludd, Mersenne, Kircher, Peter Singer and Albert von Thimus. More than half of the 53 extracts are translated into English for the first time. Godwin shows that the idea of cosmic harmony is universal, and can be a meaningful way of reading the mind of God.

HARMONIES OF HEAVEN AND EARTH
Mysticism in Music from Antiquity to the Avant-Garde
Joscelyn Godwin • 0-89281-500-0 • $12.95 paperback

Exploring music's perceived effects on matter, living things, and human behavior, Godwin shows how the spiritual power of music can be found throughout folklore, myth, and mystical experience, and includes theories of celestial harmony from Pythagoras to Marius Schneider.

> *"Through a rich, eclectic mix of mythological, philo-
> sophical, literary, and scientific references, the deeper
> meanings of sound and music are revealed."*
> Gnosis Magazine

COSMIC MUSIC

Musical Keys to the Interpretation of Reality

Joscelyn Godwin • 0-89281-070-X • $16.95 paperback

Godwin brings together three contemporary German thinkers—Marius Schneider, Rudolf Haase, and Hans Erhard Lauer—who explore the concept that the universe is created of music.

> "Cosmic Music *is the most original and exciting text currently available on the ancient musical mysteries.*"
> East West

NADA BRAHMA: THE WORLD IS SOUND

Music and the Landscape of Consciousness

Joachim-Ernst Berendt • 0-89281-168-4 • $16.95 hardcover
Also available in a paperback edition:
THE WORLD IS SOUND, 0-89281-318-0, $12.95

Producer of the highly acclaimed CD set, *Voices: A Compilation of the World's Greatest Choirs*, Berendt here takes you on an exhilarating journey through Asia, Europe, Africa, and Latin America, exploring musical traditions of many cultures and reaffirming what the ancients always knew—that the world is made of sound, rhythm, and vibration—and reveals the importance of sound in shaping cultural and spiritual life worldwide. His discussion of sound in relation to mathematics, logic, sacred geometry, myth, and sexuality is practical as well as theoretical, offering a variety of techniques for developing the ear as an organ of spiritual perception.

> "*In a majestic sweep Berendt takes the reader though the macro- and microcosm, from the 'harmony of the spheres' to the songs of dolphins and whales...*"
> from the foreword by Fritjof Capra
> Author of *The Turning Point* and *The Tao of Physics*

THE SPIRITUAL DIMENSIONS OF MUSIC

Altering Consciousness for Inner Development

R.J. Stewart • 0-89281-312-1 • $10.95 paperback

From ephemeral mood shifts to permanent transformations, music has the power to change consciousness. Through simple meditational and therapeutic exercises, Stewart explains how to approach music of all sorts—primal, environmental, individual, classical, and contemporary—through an elemental symbology that is drawn from the magical and metaphysical traditions of the West.

> *"Stewart, himself a musician and composer, presents a practical system of musical symbolism, a handbook of musical alchemy that can be applied to beneficially change our consciousness."*
> East West

THE SECRET POWER OF MUSIC

The Transformation of Self and Society Through Musical Energy

David Tame • 0-89281-056-4 • $12.95 paperback

Drawing upon the wisdom of ancient civilizations as well as contemporary scientific data, David Tame offers a challenging and timely alternative view to the widely-held modern idea that music is an intangible art form of little practical significance. He shows how music influences virtually every physical, intellectual, and emotional process, from atomic resonance to the music of the cosmos. His study of this hidden side of music may be the most detailed and all-encompassing book on the subject yet written.

THE SOUNDSCAPE

Our Sonic Environment and the Tuning of the World

R. Murray Schafer • 0-89281-455-1 • $14.95 paperback

The soundscape—a term coined by the author—is our sonic environment, the ever-present array of noises with which we all live. As civilization develops, a host of new noises rises up around us to the point that we now suffer from an overabundance of acoustic information and a proportionate diminishing of our ability to hear the nuances and subtleties of sound. The author, a well-known Canadian composer, explores our acoustic environment—past, present, and future—offering us a new awareness of the sounds around us.

> *"An unusual sensory experience...it will raise your consciousness of the soundscape to a level of sensitivity you never experienced before.*
> The New York Times

> *"It would have been timely in any age, but today it must have top priority."*
> Marshall McLuhan

THE HEALING DRUM

African Wisdom Teachings

Yaya Diallo and Mitchell Hall • 0-89281-256-7 • $12.95 paperback
The Healing Drum Audiocassette • 0-89281-264-8 • $9.95
The Healing Drum CD • 0-89281-505-1 • $14.95

Yaya Diallo tells his own intensely personal story in the first book to show the power of music as a sacred, healing force in West African culture. At a time when Africans are rapidly losing their cultural heritage to outside influences, *Lafolo Yati*—the voice of the man who speaks through the drum—tells of the depths of African spirituality and helps to preserve its timeless traditions. On the CD and audiocassette, Yaya Diallo plays the sacred and celebratory rhythms of his own Minianka tribe on authentic West African instruments.

> *"A music with powers to heal the troubled soul...Diallo [is] a complex fusion of old and new world thinking."*
> The Montreal Gazette

THE DRUMMER'S PATH

Moving the Spirit with Traditional Drumming in Performance and Invocation

Sule Greg Wilson • 0-89281-359-8 • $10.95 paperback
The Drummer's Path Audiocassette • 0-89281-362-8 • $9.95
The Drummer's Path CD • 0-89281-502-7 • $15.95

An authentic introduction to African drumming, this book is a guide to the principles and power of traditional African rhythms for all musicians and dancers. The author, who has studied and performed with many of the finest artists in the field, explains the twelve fundamental principles of invoking and executing African and Diaspora music and shows how the African spirit has been sustained by drumming and dancing. The CD and audiocassette bring together an all-star cast of international musicians in a celebration of African rhythm.

THE MAGIC FLUTE UNVEILED

Esoteric Symbolism in Mozart's Masonic Opera

Jacques Chailley • 0-89281-358-X • $14.95 paperback

This perceptive discussion of *The Magic Flute* uncovers the hidden significance of the opera's characters and situations, relating them to the esoteric traditions that inspired them, including Mozart's own involvement with Freemasonry. The author, a professor of musical history at the Sorbonne, is also the author of *40,000 Years of Music*.

These and other Inner Traditions titles are available at many fine bookstores or, to order directly from the publisher, send a check or money order for the total amount, payable to Inner Traditions, plus $3.00 shipping and handling for the first book and $1.00 for each additional book to:

Inner Traditions, P.O. Box 388, Rochester, VT 05767
Be sure to request a free catalog